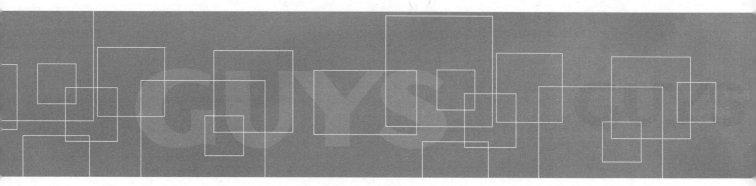

# Guys

## 10 Fearless, Faith-Focused Sessions on Issues That Matter to Guys

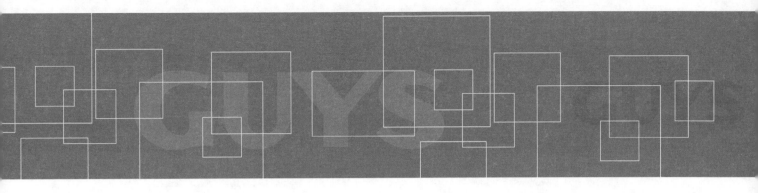

# Guys

## 10 Fearless, Faith-Focused Sessions on Issues That Matter to Guys

Dan Jessup    Helen Musick
Crystal Kirgiss

Youth Specialties

ZONDERVAN™

A DIVISION OF HARPERCOLLINS*PUBLISHERS*

*Guys: 10 Fearless, Faith-Focused Sessions on Issues That Matter to Guys*

Copyright © 2002 by Youth Specialties

Youth Specialties Books, 300 S. Pierce St., El Cajon, CA 92020, are published by Zondervan Publishing House, 5300 Patterson Ave. S.E., Grand Rapids, MI 49530.

**Library of Congress Cataloging-in-Publication Data**

Jessup, Dan, 1958-
    Guys : 10 fearless, faith-focused sessions on issues that matter to guys / Dan Jessup, Helen Musick, Crystal Kirgiss.
       p. cm.
    ISBN 0-310-24138-3
    1. Church group work with youth. 2. Boys—Religious life. I. L Musick, Helen, 1957- II. Kirgiss, Crystal. III. Title.

    BV4450 .J47 2002
    248.8'32—dc21

                                     2001039097

Web site addresses listed in this book are current at the time of publication. Please contact Youth Specialties by e-mail (YS@YouthSpecialties.com) or by postal mail (Youth Specialties, Product Department, 300 South Pierce Street, El Cajon, CA 92020) to report URLs that are not operational and to suggest alternate URLs if available.

*Edited by Vicki Newby and Dave Urbanski*
*Cover and interior design by Razdezignz*

*Printed in the United States of America*

02 03 04 05 06 07 08 / / 10 9 8 7 6 5 4 3 2 1

To my three wonderful boys, Taylor, Kevin, and Brian, who have taught me to laugh and seek the face of Jesus, and to my exceptional wife, Elizabeth, who has taught me more about love, freedom, and life than I ever dreamed could exist.

—D.J.

To my sons, Nathan and Will, as you walk through these years of self-discovery, my prayer is that your faith produces a freedom that allows you to live out God's dreams for you.

—H.M.

To Mark, a man of integrity whose passionate love for God translates into his passionate love for teens, and to our three sons, Tyler, Tory, and Tate, who are on their way to becoming men of God.

—C.K.

# Contents

A Letter from Dan Jessup . . . . . . . . . . . . . . . . . . . . . . . . . . . . . . . . . . . . . . . . . . . .9

Welcome to *Guys* . . . . . . . . . . . . . . . . . . . . . . . . . . . . . . . . . . . . . . . . . . . . . . . . . .10

1. **Your Outer Self** *How the world defines you* . . . . . . . . . . . . . . . . . . . . . . . .13

2. **Your Inner Self** *How you define you* . . . . . . . . . . . . . . . . . . . . . . . . . . . .25

3. **Your Real Self** *How God defines you* . . . . . . . . . . . . . . . . . . . . . . . . . . . .35

4. **Girls** *Decoding an alien species* . . . . . . . . . . . . . . . . . . . . . . . . . . . . . . . . .45

5. **Dating and Sexuality** *Everything you've ever wanted to know that can fit into one session* . . . . . . . . . . . . . . . . . . . . . . . . . . . . . . . . .55

6. **Blessed Are the Pure in Heart...** *For they will see God* . . . . . . . . . . . .69

7. **Friendship** *Honesty, accountability, and hangin' with the fellas* . . . . . . . . .79

8. **The Perfect Storm** *How anger can take guys by surprise* . . . . . . . . . . . . .87

9. **Wanted: Heroes** *(Super powers not required)* . . . . . . . . . . . . . . . . . . . . .97

10. **Breaking Down the Wall** *Life on the other side of today* . . . . . . . . . . . .107

# A Letter from Dan Jessup

Last week I sat with a group of seven high school sophomore guys and had the unbelievable privilege of walking them through Mark 1 where Jesus calls his first disciples. In the course of an hour, we devoured 25 pieces of chicken, one 12-pack of lukewarm Coke and every single piece of leftover Christmas candy we could find. We experienced side-splitting laughter, heart-felt prayers, and a half decent level of intelligent conversation.

As I crawled into bed that evening I couldn't help but think, "Who's going to do this for my boys when they're in high school? Who will be there to open up the Word, speak the truth, and gently or abruptly correct their self-indulged thinking? Who'll assist my wife and me when our kids begin asking those questions that help them become men?"

This book has been designed with my three boys—Taylor, Kevin, and Brian—in mind. I couldn't help but think of them. And perhaps, if this book will help someone walk alongside my sons, it might be a blessing to a few other youth workers, parents, or teachers as they walk alongside a few boys of their own.

I'd been working with kids for 11 years before I became a dad. It didn't take more that an hour or two of postpartum fatherhood for me to realize that working with kids as a youth worker and being a dad are two very different things. Clearly, being thought of as an expert in youth work was a whole lot easier than being a capable, intelligent, diaper-savvy dad! As my boys reach the teenage years, I see few good books to help me help my boys make the leap from childhood to manhood. No one can design a foolproof, all-in-one, add-water-and-stir book that will be all you need to help a boy graciously stride into adulthood. And the reality is that few books of any kind are available to assist youth workers and parents in developing our boys into young men! This book is an enthusiastic step in the direction of filling this elusive gap.

This book only introduces a handful of the issues related to becoming a man of God, but in these pages are some creative and insightful words that will assist you as you hang out with a handful of guys and address the issues of manhood without pretense or fear. And once the topics are laid on the table, opportunities for continuing discussions will present themselves. In addition to some preparation, success also requires loving relationships built between you and the boys and your prayers.

The world needs men—men who know *who* they are, men who know *whose* they are, men who aren't afraid to answer the call of Jesus in their lives, men who'll face the world with passion, love, power, faith, humility, and vision. The world is thirsty for men who will follow Jesus wherever he may lead and who will bring others along. We all want our kids to become these kind of men.

My hope and prayer is that this book gives you confidence as you help boys through the lifelong journey toward Christian manhood.

*Dan Jessup*

# ◉ WELCOME TO GUYS

10 Fearless, Faith-Focused Sessions on Issues That Matter to Guys

## Why a book for guys only?

Because, to whatever extent guys are different from other guys and girls are different from other girls, to an even greater extent, guys-as-a-whole are different from girls-as-a-whole. Our—Helen's, Dan's, and Crystal's—combined years of youth-work experience, marriage, and parenting provide endless evidence for this fact, and it was confirmed during an intense strategy and development retreat in preparation for this curriculum. Let's just say that the men and women of this team—while wholeheartedly agreeing on the purpose, topics, and goals of this book—tended to approach the discussion in, well, slightly different manners: in general, the men were more likely to crack jokes, and in general, the women were more likely to consume diet soft drinks.

Teen guys (in general, usually, as a rule, by and large, for the most part, on the whole)—

- tend to be more active than girls
- tend to be more tribal (having a large group of casual friends) than girls
- tend to be more stoic than girls
- tend to be attracted to the opposite sex based on what they see, not what they feel
- tend to like action flicks more than girls (hmm...)

...to name a few.

By framing and tailoring these lessons specifically to guys and their unique God-given design, we want to encourage your guys to ask questions, discuss, argue, learn, disagree, and offer opinions more freely than they might in a guy-girl setting.

## What's in *Guys* for you?

Each session includes the following—

### Delvin' In
Data, anecdotes, background and other stuff to get you started.

### Warmin' Up
A mixer to grab your guys' attention and get you off to a great start.

Many activities can be enhanced with appropriate music. The right tunes can add energy and enthusiasm to active games and elevate them to rockin' good times. Some activities call for soothing music that enhances reflection. Keep a CD player and selection of CDs available, and use them to your advantage.

### Diggin' a Little Deeper
Your choice of group, video, or individual activities, each intended to draw your guys into the topic and explore it. Use one. Use any two. Use all three.

### Gettin' into the Word
A study of God's Word directly related to the topic.

The Gettin' into the Word Bible study includes a list of Nudgers. What are they? Thoughts, ideas, prompts, and questions to help you and your group think about the Bible more deeply. Here are some ways to use them—

*For the leaders—*
Read through the Bible passage and Nudgers throughout the week preceding the lesson to get your own creative and insightful thoughts flowing.

*For the guys—*

- After introducing the Bible passage, read Nudgers to your guys while their eyes are closed, encouraging them to visualize and think about the story in a new way.
- Read appropriate Nudgers before each individual discussion question.
- Print copies of Nudgers for all your students to reflect on while the Bible passage is being read.
- During the lesson give each guy one Nudger to reflect on. Let your guys share their thoughts with the group.
- In pairs, have the guys read the Nudgers one at a time and discuss them together.
- Make copies of Nudgers for your guys to take home and think about during the week.

## Takin' It to Heart
A wrap-up activity and prayer.

## Quotes
Quotes taken from the Bible and contemporary sources, the topic-relevant quotes are scattered throughout the lessons. Use them to prompt your own reflection, post them in your room, or draw them into the discussions.

## The Next Step
A handout to help your teens process the activities and discussion.

Offer an example or two of key ideas, especially during the first few sessions so your guys understand what you're looking for. Pick one of the key ideas and let the guys offer suggestions for action steps.

Here are several ideas for processing The Next Step with your group. You may want to vary the way you handle this activity from session to session.

- Let the group brainstorm ideas for the top half; record them on a whiteboard. Have each guy choose one idea and write action steps for himself. Have everyone share his action steps with the group or a partner.
- Let the guys fill out the top half individually; have them share their ideas with the group; let the guys fill out the bottom half individually (selecting a new idea if they want); let the boys share their action steps with the group.
- Have everyone fill out the handout individually. Share the circled idea or action plan or both with the group or with a partner.

Encourage your teens to keep the worksheet handy during the week—in their Bibles, in school notebooks, next to their beds, on bulletin boards in their rooms—so they can be reminded to pray for God's help and to do the action steps they listed.

## We've added something new!

All the handouts in Guys are posted at www.YouthSpecialties.com/free/guys, where you can access them for free!

- **Plain Text** Just plain ol' text. Format- and graphic-free so you can change the words or add new design. Accessible no matter what computer or word-processing program you own.
- **Rich Text Format** Customizable text (no graphics) with basic formatting such as bold and italics.
- **MS Word 95/6.0** Customizable text (no graphics) with basic formatting such as bold and italics.

- **Adobe PDF** The designed handout as it appears in this book (not customizable). Print one copy to take to the copier or print all the copies you need for your group on your computer's printer.

## Preparation: Ya gotta love it!

These sessions are guidelines for you—ideas, suggestions, and possibilities. We know a thing or two about guys as a whole, but we don't know your kids. You know your guys best, what activities will work with them, what concepts need emphasis, how active they need to be, how closely they've already bonded. So tweak, add, delete, substitute, or adjust our ideas to make them your own.

Of course, you can manage this best when you plan and prepare in advance. We've tried to help you, to make it easy for you. But if you read the material in the car on the way to the meeting, you're bound to experience some disappointments. Enhance your ministry to teen guys by reading the sessions in advance and spending a bit of time preparing.

## Keeping your perspective

A lot of information is available about youth ministry—what it is, how to do it, how to do it better, how to survive it, and how to succeed at it. We'd like to boil it down for you to a few simple thoughts—

- Ministry is not a thing, a theory, or a theology. It's a way of life.
- Ministry is not something you're trained to do (though training is well and good). It's something you're born, or rather reborn, to do.
- Ministry is not something that happens at youth group, at the high school, or during ministry hours. It's something that happens everywhere, all the time.
- Ministry is not about what you do. It's about who you serve.
- Ministry is simply this…loving God and loving others.

Peace from all of us,

*Crystal Kirgiss*

### ◉ TIP

The final session (week 10) is a time for celebrating, a time for affirming, a time for blessing. Even as you begin to read through the first session, look ahead to Session 10. Give yourself plenty of time to pull together a support team and to plan a memorable event.

# 1 Your Outer Self
## How the world defines you

## ⊘ THE ISSUE

Though the world pays lip service to the concept of guys "getting in touch with their emotions," the fact remains that guys in general are encouraged to be rough, tough, macho, and even sexist. Christian guys need to recognize the difference between being tough and being strong.

---

### introduction
## Delvin' In

Check out the psychology and parenting sections next time you're in a bookstore and you'll find countless books written on the perils of being a teenage girl. Unrealistic definitions of beauty. Unrealistic expectations of body size and shape. Unrealistic guidelines for success. Valid issues, all of them.

But what about being a teenage boy—does it carry its own and equally lethal doses of false messages and unrealistic expectations? And if so, does the resulting sense of inadequacy felt by many teen guys need to be addressed?

Absolutely.

Our culture says guys must be buff, must be athletic, must cause the girls to swoon, must not be weak, must not let anyone walk on them, must aggressively pursue goals, must conquer a female, must be tough.

It takes a lot of courage to stand firm against false and shallow definitions of success, masculinity, and power, especially now when teens are constantly in touch with our culture through the entertainment media and the Internet. Whether they realize it or not, our culture's standard of manhood gets about a thousand times more of their attention than God's standard. In order to help teen guys pursue a life of authentic manhood, they must first identify and recognize our culture's false definition of manhood. In this case, ignorance is not bliss. Ignorance is a world full of self-centered, egotistical, macho tough guys.

### opening activity
## Warmin' Up

**Who Am I?**

Write the names of well-known males on the index cards—one name on each card. You can use athletes, musicians, actors, politicians, authors, local celebrities. The names should all be familiar to your guys. If you have a group of five or less, have one teen come to the front. Then tape one name card on the wall behind him so that the others can see it but he can't. Explain the activity like this—

> **You'll need—**
> • Index cards or small pieces of paper
> • Masking tape
> • Marker

*The card I just hung up has the name of a famous male on it. [Name of teen] has to figure out whose name is on the card. He may only ask yes-or-no questions. He can direct his questions to the entire group or to any individual in the group. His goal is to name the person in as few questions as possible.*

**⊙ TIP**
If the student up front is having a hard time even after asking a number of questions, give a leading hint like, "This person is a musician" or "This person died about 10 years ago." Give a helpful hint but don't make it too specific.

If you have a group of six or more, tape an index card with a name written on it onto the back of each guy. Then give an explanation like this—

> *Each of you has the name of a famous male taped on your back. It's your job to figure out who he is by asking each other yes-or-no questions. For example, you can ask, "Is my person an athlete?" but you may not ask, "What kind of work does he do?" Once you've asked one question, you can answer one question. Then you have to move to a different person.*

Let the students mingle for several minutes while asking questions. When each person has figured out his name (or after 10 minutes), pull your group together and ask questions like these.

> ➤ What kind of questions were most helpful in identifying your person (questions about occupation? appearance? age?)?
> ➤ What makes your person famous?
> ➤ What do you admire about your person?
> ➤ If your person is well-liked, what do you think draws people to him?

## exploring the topic
# Diggin' a Little Deeper

Transition with something like this—

> *One of the main ways we identify people is by appearance and by occupation. Almost everyone knows the name of the most recent winning quarterback of the Super Bowl. Far fewer know who discovered the polio vaccine.*
>
> *What makes some people famous and others unknown? In the case of women, the world usually worships beauty over individuality. "She's a brilliant politician, but she's not much to look at." Ever heard something like*

*that before? In the case of men, one of the fame factors is toughness. "Did you see him take down those two defensive linemen even though he's playing with a broken hand?"*

*The world's idea of what makes a man valuable is shallow: How much money does he make? How many coworkers can he step on as he climbs the ladder to success? Can he take care of himself in a fight? Can he survive difficult situations without looking weak, showing fear, or—worst of all—shedding tears?*

*Let's take a look at how the world identifies and defines men.*

Choose one or more of the following activities.

option [group activity]
Mirror, Mirror, on the Wall, Who's the Toughest of Them All?

Divide your guys into groups of three or four. Explain to them that you're going to take a look at how the world portrays men. Hand out several newspaper sections, pens, and one copy of **Mirror, Mirror, on the Wall, Who's the Toughest of Them All?** (page 20) to each group. Give them about 10 minutes to look through the papers (encourage them to look through a variety of sections, not just sports or entertainment) and fill out the worksheet as a group. When the groups have their lists made, come together and discuss the results with some questions.

## You'll need—

- A stack of recent newspapers
- Copies of **Mirror, Mirror, on the Wall, Who's the Toughest of Them All?** (page 20), one for each group
- Pens

- Based on what you observed, what are the characteristics our culture admires or glorifies in men? Explain.
- If someone doesn't have those characteristics, how is he perceived? Talk about that.
- What characteristics define toughness besides the physical aspects?
- Think of a man you admire who is not a tough guy (as our culture defines it). Why do you admire him?

option [video clip discussion]
## Billy Madison

Show the clip from *Billy Madison* where Billy tries to fit in and make his mark as a smooth dude on his first day of high school.

**0:54:55** Billy pulls up to the school in his sportster.

**0:57:19** "Are you in loser denial or something?" [*warning*: bad language follows quickly—you may want to have your finger on the stop button]

Ask questions like these—

- Why do you think guys care about the tough-guy, macho image so much?
- Do you think guys are better off being themselves (even if others view them as losers, wimps, or thumbs-down guys) or acting tough and macho, no matter what? Talk about that.
- Why are some guys so cruel to others whom they think are weak? Explain.

It wasn't so long ago that you were mired in that old stagnant life of sin. You let the world, which doesn't know the first thing about living, tell you how to live.
—*from Ephesians 2,* The Message

option [second video clip discussion]
## Commercial Break

**TIP**
**This takes some prep time. It's easy to do, but don't delay!**

During the week, make a video recording of "guy" commercials. The best time to do this is during sporting events and cop shows. (Sounds sexist, but hey, that's the Madison Avenue way.) Try to capture a variety of guy personalities—tough, goofy, comedic, professional, intelligent. Record 10 to 15 ads.

**You'll need—**
- Taped commercials (see instructions below)
- TV and VCR

Introduce the activity with a comment like this—

*One of the ways our thinking about being a guy is influenced is from the entertainment media, especially television. We're going to watch some commercials that feature guys in a variety of situations and then figure out what they say about us as men.*

Play the tape. Then ask some of these questions.

- Describe the different kinds of men in the ads.
- How accurately do they represent real men? Explain your thinking.
- How did the tough guys act? The nerdy guys? The married guys? The stupid guys? The sexist guys?
- Did any of the ads create a feeling of genuine respect for men? Which ones and why?
- How do you think the idea that guys should be tough began? Talk about that.

"By the early 1990s, the image of Marky Mark in his briefs—including the parts that were concealed but definitely suggested—posed a challenge to young men everywhere. And few could measure up. Even as competitive sports were becoming a somewhat less important part of high school boys' lives, competitive bodies were becoming more important. Moreover, the ideal male body type was not, as it had traditionally been, a normal by-product of athletics, work, and physical activity. Rather, it was something to be consciously achieved through exercise intended to make the body conform to an aesthetic ideal."

*—Thomas Hine in* The Rise and Fall of the American Teenager
*(Avon, 1999, page 289)*

"perfect" profile. How do you think he deals with life, with the way others view him, and with the way others treat him? Explain.

**option [second individual activity]**
Tough as Nails,
Strong as Steel

Each student needs a copy of **Tough as Nails, Strong as Steel** (page 22), a Bible, and a pen. Open with a few comments.

**You'll need—**
• Copies of **Tough as Nails, Strong as Steel** (page 22), one for each student
• Bibles
• Pens

**option [individual activity]**
Thumbs Up, Thumbs Down

Give each guy a copy of **Thumbs Up, Thumbs Down** (page 21) and a pen. For the Thumbs Up side, your kids describe the perfect guy according to our culture, including physical, intellectual, and behavioral traits. For the Thumbs Down side, they describe the traits of a loser as seen by our culture.

**You'll need—**
• Copies of **Thumbs Up, Thumbs Down** (page 21), one for each student

When they've finished, ask for some volunteers to share their answers. Then discuss some of the following questions.

➤ Do most people buy into our culture's definitions of a perfect guy and a loser? Why do you think that?

➤ If someone wants to be "perfect," how does this affect his actions, personality, and decisions? Talk about your thoughts.

➤ If people see a guy as a loser, how is his life affected? Give some examples (without naming names).

➤ Think of someone who ignores the world's message about male identity. He's confident and content with himself. But according to the world, he's closer to the "loser" profile than the

*There are many different ways to describe men. You've probably heard "tough as nails" and "strong as steel." They sound the same, but they're really very different. "Tough as nails" men do exactly what their title says— they pound into, pierce, and wound others with their words and actions. They try to prove that they're tough by hurting others. What they're really doing, though, is trying to feel better about themselves—hiding their weaknesses, their insecurities, their fears—by harassing or dominating others, male or female. The only way they know how to move up in the world is by taking others down.*

*"Strong as steel" men are just the opposite. Steel is used to construct buildings because it doesn't weaken under pressure. It doesn't bend. It doesn't twist. It remains constant under all conditions. Because of that, the building is strong.*

*Tough guys tear other people down. Strong men support others. Tough guys delight in another's failure. Strong men delight in another's success. Tough guys want to rise to the top and be noticed. Strong men are content to be part of the whole (often unseen), holding things together with their sturdy commitment.*

Give your teens several minutes to look up the Bible verses and think about the differences between tough guys and strong men. Then ask some follow-up questions.

> ➤ Do you agree with the definitions of tough guy and strong men on your handout? Explain your thoughts.
> ➤ How do you think tough guys feel about themselves? Explain.
> ➤ Are strong men noticed or appreciated by others? Talk about that.
> ➤ What kind of man does our culture prefer? Explain why you think so.
> ➤ What kind of man does God prefer? Explain why you think so.
> ➤ What other examples of tough guys and strong men can you identify from the Bible?

## Bible study
# Gettin' into the Word

**King Saul and King David**
1 Samuel, selected verses

Transition into the next activity by saying something like this.

**You'll need—**
• Bibles

*For whatever reason, the world seems to think that tough guys are all that. The combination of looks, physical strength, and machismo seems to captivate people. In the short run, many tough guys come out ahead. Since we're a society that's all about immediate gratification, it's easy to do the tough-guy thing without thinking about the long-range consequences. We're going to look at a tough guy from the Bible to see how things worked out for him.*

 **Nudgers** (nuj´erz) *n.* a tool used to gently push teens toward new insight

> ➤ Saul's father was well known.
> ➤ David's father was not well known.
> ➤ Saul was considered impressive because of his physical appearance, in particular his height.
> ➤ David was not tall.
> ➤ Saul was a warrior and king.
> ➤ David was a shepherd, a lowly occupation.
> ➤ Saul's courage was based on himself and

> was a cover for a lack of character.
> ➤ David's courage was based on God's strength and was genuine.
> ➤ Saul, the mighty warrior, watched while David, the shepherd boy, killed Goliath.
> ➤ Saul's contribution to the heroic event? The offer of a free armor loan.

Goliath walked out toward David with his shield bearer ahead of him, sneering in contempt at this ruddy-faced boy. "Am I a dog," he roared at David, "that you come at me with a stick?" And he cursed David by the names of his gods. "Come over here, and I'll give your flesh to the birds and wild animals!"
—*1 Samuel 17:41-44, NLT*

Have your students read the following verses.

**Saul** I Samuel 9:1-2; 10:1, 23; 15:17, 30
**David** I Samuel 16:1, 6-12; 17:1-7, 32-33, 38-50

Then discuss the following questions.

> Do you think the Israelites based their judgments of Saul and David on appearance, character, or both? Talk about that.
> Goliath was a perfect match for the tough, macho, manly guy description. Why do you think Goliath-types feel the need to harass those who are smaller and weaker? Explain your thinking.
> How do guys react when being harassed by Goliath-types?
> Do most guys prefer to be a Goliath-type (tough, bully), Saul-type (attractive, powerful, leader) or a David-type (quiet, unknown, self-confident)? Explain.

But the Lord said to Samuel, "Do not consider his appearance or his height, for I have rejected him. The Lord does not look at the things man looks at. Man looks at the outward appearance, but the Lord looks at the heart."

—I Samuel 16:7

Conclude with something like this—

*Our culture has a lot of opinions about people—how they should act, what they should look like, who they should hang out with, and what makes them acceptable. In the Bible passage we looked at today, we see the difference between what our culture thinks and what God thinks. Saul was a king—powerful and wealthy. David was a shepherd—young and untrained. Yet David, not Saul, had the courage to take on Goliath because—*

> *David was defending God's honor, not his own.*
> *David trusted in the Lord. He was willing to put his life on the line because he remembered the past when God had protected him.*

> *David knew the Lord had prepared him for this battle through his life experiences.*
> *David didn't feel pressure to fight the battle with conventional weapons. He knew his success would come from the Lord, not from his weapons or his strength.*
> *David didn't come to fight. He came to serve.*

*Late in David's life he became a great warrior, winning battle after battle in the name of the Lord. David's life— from shepherd to giant killer to warrier—is a model of how God can work in our lives, making us into men who draw our strength from him. In time and with some experience, we can all develop David's confidence in the Lord.*

# Takin' It to Heart

Give everyone a copy of **The Next Step— Becoming a Man of Strength** (page 23) Share an example or two of key ideas if you like. Allow some time

**You'll need—**

• Copies of **The Next Step— Becoming a Man of Strength** (page 23), one for each guy
• Pens

to fill out the handouts and review their responses. Remind them to keep their papers where they can review them during the week.

Close in prayer, perhaps with thoughts like—

*Dear God,
You know how hard it is to grow up in this world. We get all kinds of conflicting messages about what it means to be a man. Please help us to*

*be the kind of men you want us to be. We want to see our weaknesses and draw from your strength. We want to be used by you like David was. Amen.*

 **TIP**

**Look ahead to Session 10, Breaking Down the Wall. To have a special closing celebration, allow plenty of time for planning, delegating, organizing, and preparing.**

All handouts are posted at
www.YouthSpecialties.com/free/guys
in plain text, Rich Text Format,
MS Word 95/6.0, and PDF formats.
Buyers of *Guys* can use them for *free!*

All quotes in this book that are denoted by age are from *Live and Learn and Pass It On*, by H. Jackson Brown Jr., (Nashville, Tennessee: Rutledge Hill Press, 1991, 1992). Reprinted by permission.

# Mirror, Mirror, on the Wall, Who's the Toughest of Them All?

Glance through the headlines in the newspaper looking for names of well-known men. List them below in the appropriate column. Put one of these letters next to each name.

**S** strong

**I** intelligent

**F** funny

**A** athletic

**H** helpful

**T** talented

| Politicians | Businessmen | Actors/Musicians/ Authors | Athletes | Other |
|---|---|---|---|---|
| | | | | |
| | | | | |
| | | | | |
| | | | | |
| | | | | |
| | | | | |
| | | | | |
| | | | | |
| | | | | |
| | | | | |
| | | | | |
| | | | | |
| | | | | |
| | | | | |
| | | | | |

# THUMBS UP, THUMBS DOWN

## THUMBS UP
Describe the man our culture applauds.

## THUMBS DOWN
Describe the man our culture rejects.

Tough guys do whatever it takes to *appear tough on the outside* so they can cover up the weaknesses and insecurity they feel on the inside.

Strong men do whatever it takes to *be right on the inside* so they can live obediently in spite of whatever weakness and insecurities they may have.

# TOUGH AS NAILS, STRONG AS STEEL

Read Exodus 1:8-22. Note how these characters acted.

**TOUGH AS NAILS**

**Who is tough?**

**Who is weak?**

**PHAROH**

**SLAVEMASTERS**

**ISRAELITES**

**HEBREW MIDWIVES**

Read John 8:1-11. Note how these characters acted.

**STRONG AS STEEL**

**Who is obedient?**

**Who is strong?**

**PHARISEES**

**THE WOMEN**

**OLDER TEACHERS OF THE LAW**

**JESUS**

Think about the lesson we've just finished. List four or five key ideas that stand out the most.

1. _____

2. _____

3. _____

4. _____

5. _____

Which idea on your list is the most important to you? Circle it.

## Take Action

What are specific actions or steps you can take to make your circled idea a reality?

1. _____

2. _____

3. _____

# THE ISSUE

When the day is done, when the buddies have all gone home, when a young man sits in solitude behind a door that closes out social and family life, who is he…really? Not only are guys encouraged to uphold a tough exterior, but they're also taught to keep their feelings to themselves. Guys need a chance to search for the unique individual that God created… without fear of ridicule or rejection.

introduction
## Delvin' In

So you've made it through the first session. Hopefully, your guys have begun to recognize the world's doctrine of identity—"Be tough (rich, athletic, successful, et cetera, et cetera, et cetera) and you'll do just fine." Hopefully, your guys understand that the world's message isn't a truthful one. Hopefully, your guys would like to dig a little deeper and discover the "real me" that lives in each one of them. Wouldn't it be great if you could just bring all your guys into a cozy room, serve some cookies and milk, and say, "Okay, now tell me how you *really* feel"?

If only it could be that easy. Or that fast.

Helping teens compile a truthful and realistic picture of themselves is hard enough, with all the

quote

"You are unique. You are a human being, but you are not just any human being. In all the history of mankind there never has been, nor will there ever be, a person exactly like you. You have feelings and thoughts that no one else has ever felt or thought before. You have a unique dignity: of all the millions of people that God might have created in place of you, he chose to create you."
— *Vincent P. Collins in* Me, Myself and You *(Abbey Press, 1974, page 103)*

media influences and technological advances. Helping *guy* teens is another challenge entirely.

We often assume that girls suffer more roadblocks than boys when it comes to growing up and developing into an individual. But that's

not so. In his book, *The Wonder of Boys* (Tarcher/Putnam, 1996), Michael Gurian writes—

For the last few decades our cultural microscope has focused on the oppression of girls and women. That focus has led us to many gains in public consciousness, national policy, and private life. Now the lens must focus on boys too. For every boy who feels powerful at home or in his neighborhood there is another boy who feels lost. For every football star there are far more male drug addicts, teenage alcoholics, high school dropouts, and juvenile delinquents. Boys are in pain.

He suggests that in order to make any progress in understanding young people, we must stop believing the stereotype that "boys lead more privileged lives." In fact, both genders have their own unique privileges. Boys, in general, have more physical power, a wider variety of job opportunities (or extracurricular activities), and more encouragement from adults to "be all that they can be." Girls, in general, receive more nurturing and personal protection and have a longer lifespan.

So who's to say that being a boy is easier? In some ways, yes. In other ways, no.

Boys may be receiving a subtle message of "you can do everything, go anywhere, and be anything you want to." But is it true?

Do parents fervently encourage boys who want to be nurses or do they say, "Why not be a doctor, instead?" How about the budding musician? Does he hear adults say, "That's so awesome that you can write your own music!" or "But how are you going to pay the rent?" The young man who loves children and wants to be a kindergarten teacher—does the world view him as a sane and rational human being who has extraordinary skills relating to young children, or is he considered a namby-pamby who's too stupid to become a high school science teacher and too clumsy to coach varsity football?

Sure, boys have certain advantages based on their physical build and mental wiring, but they still have to wade through the murky waters known as, "What and who do I want to be when I grow up?"

## opening activity
# Warmin' Up

### And in This Corner...

Before you begin, mark off a space in the middle of the room (using tape, chairs, cones, or whatever else you might have on hand) to be No Man's Land. If you want your students to have plenty of personal space, make No Man's Land resemble Texas. If you want them to enjoy each other's cramped and cozy company for a few brief moments, make No Man's Land resemble Deleware.

**quote**

"I've learned that you shouldn't compare yourself to the best others can do, but to the best you can do."
—age 68

This game is all about recognizing unique and quirky characteristics and letting your guys move around. Give each corner of the room a number (you can post a sign if you want) and describe the game like this—

*Starting at the back left corner and moving clockwise we have Corner 1, Corner 2, Corner 3, and Corner 4. I'm going to call out certain char-acteristics, interests, and abilities, and you move to the appropriate corner as fast as possible. Sometimes you'll only choose between going to a certain corner or not. Sometimes you'll have to choose between two different corners. If you don't fit the description, move to No-Man's-Land, which is here in the middle.*

### ◎ TIP

If your guys crave competition, you can add some elimination rules such as—

- **The first five into any corner remain in play. The rest are out.**
- **The last one into No Man's Land is out.**

Use the following list of ideas. Note that some are single choices, some are double. Add whatever comes to mind that's appropriate for your group or skip what your group might not relate to. This is your chance to shine the spotlight on your killer accordion player or that national pig-calling champion. The goals of the activity are to get your guys moving and to let them see that there's almost always at least one other person who is like them in one way or another.

➤ If you're left-handed, go to corner 2; if you're right-handed, go to corner 4.
➤ If you've ever blown soda pop out your nose while laughing, go to corner 3.
➤ If you watch professional wrestling, go to corner 1.
➤ If you think professional wrestling is real, go to corner 2.
➤ If you plan on going to college, go to corner 3; if you want to start work right after high school, go to corner 1.
➤ If you like football more than basketball, go to corner 2; if you like basketball more than football, go to corner 3; if you like soccer best, go to corner 4.
➤ If you play in band or sing in choir, go to corner 1.
➤ If you're a member of an athletic team, go to corner 4.
➤ If you serve on student council, go to corner 2.

- If you can turn your eyelids inside out, go to corner 3.
- If you've ever had stitches, go to corner 1.
- If you can suck dental floss into your nose and out your mouth, go to corner 4.
- If you've gotten a speeding ticket, go to corner 2.
- If you like hard rock best, go to corner 1; if you like R&B and rap best, go to corner 2; if you like alternative and modern rock best, go to corner 3; if you like ska and punk best, go to corner 4; if you don't like any of the choices, go to the middle.
- If you know what career you want to pursue, go to corner 3.

## ⦿ TIP

**If you'd rather have an up-front-and-visible activity, invite volunteers to demonstrate unique talents—stupid human tricks—to the group: double-jointed elbows, jiggling eyes, a tongue that reaches into a nostril, and so on.**

When you've finished, move into the next section with something like—

*Everyone deals with the pressure of conformity—being, acting, dressing, and talking like everyone else. But who wants to live in a world like that? Everyone else would essentially be you and you would be everyone else. That would make for pretty boring conversation, competition, and relationships. God made each of us marvelously unique. He gave us those differences for a purpose, and he doesn't want you to be embarrassed or ashamed of who you really are.*

*So the question is this: do you know who you really are? We're going to try and find out.*

## exploring the topic
# Diggin' a Little Deeper

Choose one of the following activities.

option [group activity]
### The Final Four

Before you begin this activity, write the following list of attributes and values on the whiteboard.

**You'll need—**
- A whiteboard or piece of butcher paper
- A marker
- Blank paper, one for each student
- 4 sticky notes for each student
- Pens

INTEGRITY
PHYSICAL HEALTH
WELL-PAYING CAREER
MARRIAGE AND FAMILY
SPIRITUAL MATURITY
CREATIVITY
KNOWLEDGE
FRIENDSHIP
OPPORTUNITY TO VOLUNTEER

CHURCH
SEXUAL PURITY
SOCIAL JUSTICE
COURAGE
SPORTS
WISDOM

Make sure the list is large enough for everyone to see it clearly. Give each student a blank piece of paper and pen. Say something like this—

*This list includes many things that are probably important to all of you. Each thing is good and valuable in its own way. It would be nice to pursue and actually have all of the things on the list. But life isn't like that. Even if every team in a tournament is great, only two can move to the finals. Even if every album nominated for a Grammy is spectacular, only one is chosen.*

*We all have choices to make. We all have to decide what things are most important. If we spread ourselves too thin by trying to do and have it all, we might end up with nothing.*

*Look at this list and decide which 10 things you would be most willing to work hard for, maybe even make big sacrifices to have. Write those 10 things on your piece of paper.*

> You're blessed when you're content with just who you are—no more, no less. That's the moment you find yourselves proud owners of everything that can't be bought.
> —*Jesus, from Matthew 5,* The Message

Give the students a few minutes to do this. They should make their choices alone, but the room doesn't need to be silent. If they want to ask questions or bounce ideas off each other, let them. When they've had a chance to finish this, ask for a volunteer to read his list. Then continue—

> **Now look at your top 10 choices and narrow those down to six. Be sure the six you choose are very valuable to you, worth the investment of energy and time that they might require.**

Ignore any complaining. Let them work on this for a few minutes, ask for a few volunteers to read their lists, and then go at them again.

> **Even though you've already narrowed down your list to six things, chances are that you'll only be able to actively pursue three or four things. Along the way, you might attain some more of your goals, but it won't happen all at once. Choose the four things on your list that are absolutely the most important to you and circle those now.**

Ask each teen to read his Final Four (though don't force anyone). This isn't a test, so don't criticize or offer commentary on anyone's choices. Don't make anyone feel that he's made a bad or wrong choice. When they've finished, give them one last challenge—to narrow their lists to *the* single most important item.

Make sure your students feel comfortable following their own instincts. You don't want anyone to feel that God *must* be their number one choice just because they're in youth group or church or a discipleship group. That would be nice, but obviously your guys are all at different places in their lives. View this as an opportunity to see inside their hearts.

Give each guy four sticky notes. Tell them to write each of their Final Four on a separate note and number them from one (most important) to four (least important of the four). They can stick the notes inside one of the covers of their Bibles. Or they can stick their    notes to a spot on the wall as a visible reminder of the choices they made.

Then ask these questions—

> ➤ How did you make your decisions as we went further along in the narrowing process? Explain.
> ➤ Why might it be helpful for you in the future to have identified the things you value the most? Explain.
> ➤ Have you decided on the five things you value the most or has someone else—like your parents, friends, school, church—imposed them on you? Talk about that.
> ➤ How might identifying the things you value affect your daily life? Your decisions? Your friends? Your relationships with your family? What you want to do with your life after school?

**quote**

"I've learned that when I grow up, I'm going to be an artist. It's in my blood."

—*age 8*

Close this activity with something like this—

> **This week, think of a way that you can remember your Final Four. Write them down in a place where you'll see them regularly. That list is a vital reflection of the real you—what you value, what you believe in, what you're willing to pursue. You're much more than the world will ever realize, so don't let the world define you.**

option [video clip discussion]
**October Sky**

Homer, the son of a coal miner, dreams of building rockets. Play the video clip in which Homer, after spending some time working in the mines, finally gets up the nerve to tell his dad that he's not going to follow in the family footsteps. He's going to pursue his dream instead.

**1:17:31** A book is open to a diagram of a rocket.
**1:20:00** Homer's father walks up the stairs.

You can ask questions like these—

➤ Are you afraid of telling people what you really want to do and be? Why or why not?
➤ What expectations are put on guys in terms of their futures? How do those expectations affect your plans and hopes?
➤ If a guy wants to pursue a dream that others think is unrealistic, what roadblocks do you think he'll face?
➤ How do you think he should deal with those roadblocks?

**quote**

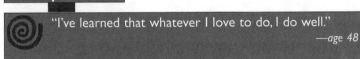

"I've learned that whatever I love to do, I do well."
—age 48

option [individual activity]
**In My Mind's Eye**

Begin with something like this—

**You'll need—**
• Copies of **In My Mind's Eye** (page 33), one for each student
• Pens

*One of the most frightening things that teens face is an unknown future. Will you go to college? If so, where? What will it be like there? What kind of job will you pursue? Will you find someone to marry? Will you have kids? Where do you want to live? What do you really want to be? Will that ever happen?*

*There's no way for you to know what tomorrow holds, let alone what your life will be like 10 years down the road. God promises that he has a plan for you, but that doesn't make the future less mysterious. One of the most common fears among young Christians—though few will admit it—is this: "If I give God total control of my life, he'll send me to Africa to be a missionary. Or he'll make me preach on street corners. Or he'll never let me fall in love with a woman. He'll ruin my life!"*

*You all know those fears aren't true, but you might worry about them anyway.*

*Listen to these encouraging words, written by a mature Christian man, that offer a different way of thinking about God's plans for your future:*

**How can a young man find his true place in life? Is there any way he can discover what God really wants him to be and do? Almost every young man hopes that his future holds some splendid purpose.**

**But you might feel like a plain, everyday sort of person who could never have an exciting and splendid life.** *How can there be something wonderful in my future? And if there is, how can I possibly figure out what it is?*

**The answer is simple: already in your past life, from time to time, God himself has whispered into your heart just that very wonderful thing, whatever it is, that he is wishing you to be and to do and to have. And that wonderful thing is nothing less than what is called your *heart's desire*. Nothing less than that. The most secret, sacred wish that lies deep down at the bottom of your heart, the wonderful thing that you hardly dare to look at or to think about— the thing that you would rather die**

than have anyone else know of, because it seems so far beyond anything that you are or have at the present time, that you fear that you would be cruelly ridiculed if the mere thought of it were known—that is just the very thing that God is wishing you to do or to be for him.

And the birth of that marvelous wish in your soul—the dawning of that secret dream—was the Voice of God himself telling you to arise and come up higher because he has need of you.*

Give each student a copy of **In My Mind's Eye** (page 33) and a pen. Then say—

*For just a minute, I want you to think about your deepest desire for your life. I'm not talking about the beautiful girl in your history class or the new Porsche your dentist drives.*

*I'm talking about who you want to be and what you want to do. Maybe you've never told anyone else.*

*Right now, I want you to write it on your paper. I want you to pray about it for a few moments, and then I want you to put the paper away. Fold it up and put it in your pocket. Toss it in the trash. Stick it in your Bible. Keep it private. It's just for you to know.*

*Someday you might want to talk about it. But tonight, I just want you to name it.*

Give the guys a few minutes to do this. Remember, guys are usually action- and task-oriented. This activity may be a stretch for them. They might even have a blank look on their faces. You're actually giving them a gift—a private moment of silence to be totally honest with themselves.

* Adapted from *Your Heart's Desire* by Emmet Fox (DeVorss Publications, 1933).

⊙ **TIP**

If you have guys who are really interested in self-discovery or guys who are older and quickly approaching independence, check out *Find Your Fit: Dare to Act on God's Design for You* by Jane Kise and Kevin Johnson (Bethany House, 1998) and *Find Your Fit: Dare to Act on Who You Are Discovery Workbook* (1999). These resources deal with talents, interests, spiritual gifts, and personality traits.

When your students are finished, ask the following questions—

> ➤ Does your dream for the future seem possible? Why or why not?
> ➤ What do you think your parents, friends and teachers would say about your future dreams? Explain.
> ➤ How do you see God being involved in your future dreams? Explain.
> ➤ What things can you do now to start preparing for the future, whatever it may hold?

─ Bible study ─
# Gettin' into the Word

**David Mourns for His Child**
2 Samuel 12:13-23

Move into the Bible study with something like this—

*Because there's so much pressure in today's world to be and look a certain way, people don't always feel comfortable showing their hopes, fears, and emotions. This is especially true of guys. In our culture guys must display a tough-guy, composed mask. No sadness, no fear, no insecurity allowed. And above all, no crying, please.*

*It's impossible to live your entire life with two different personalities—*

*the inner and the outer—without falling apart, cracking up, or getting an ulcer. Let's take a look at a guy in the Bible who followed his instincts and showed his inner feelings, even when others might have ridiculed or abandoned him.*

 **Nudgers** (nuj´erz) *n.* a tool used to gently push teens toward new insight

➤ David was considered to be the mightiest warrior of his day.
➤ David was hugely popular with citizens of Israel.
➤ David's behavior was "unmanly."
➤ David's actions embarrassed others, even his own servants.
➤ David's display of weakness affected how his servants viewed him.

➤ David's actions seemed irrational and ridiculous to others.
➤ David acted in accordance with his heart and with logical thinking.
➤ David's household wanted him to stop mourning when he was sad and to mourn when he refreshed himself.

Provide a brief recap of the events leading up to the passage (David's sin with Bathsheba, death of Uriah, Nathan's rebuke). Then read 2 Samuel 12:13-23 to your students.

**⊙ TIP**

If you have a few willing students, ask one to read Nathan's words, another to read David's, and another to read the servants'. You, or another student, read all the remaining lines, serving as a narrator.

When you've finished reading, say something like—

*David was Israel's golden king. His subjects loved and adored him. He was known for his mighty battles and numerous victories. He was a strong policy maker. He was handsome, rich, powerful, and well-liked. It seems a man like that would be careful about*

*protecting and preserving his image. But David was nothing if not poetic, emotional, and honest with his feelings. Just read a few psalms if you need convincing. It's hard to imagine a president, a prime minister, or any other world leader displaying such emotions in a completely honest and genuine way. But not for David. He was transparent and never let his public image control his inner identity.*

Ask the following questions—

➤ How did others react to David's display of emotion? What might David's servants have thought of him?
➤ Those around David questioned his actions not once, but twice. What do you think that says about him?
➤ If you've ever been in a situation that stirs your emotions, how have you acted or reacted?
➤ Is it more difficult for guys to reveal their inner identity than it is for girls? Why or why not?
➤ Do you think society's way of doing things (big boys don't cry) or David's way (pass the tissues please) is better? Think beyond crying. Include fears, worries, dreams, hopes, joys, sorrows—in other words, how is it better to honor the inner person than to hide the inner person?
➤ What might make it easier for guys to be honest about what they think and feel? Explain why.
➤ Is it possible for someone to be too open and honest? Give an example or explain.

Close the lesson with something like this—

*God created you as a unique individual. He is not in the business of creating robots, clones, or mass-produced human beings. If the world were a band, he wouldn't want all the members to be lead guitarists. If it were a basketball team, he wouldn't want all the players to be centers. If that were the case, he could have created a single person and been done with it.*

*God has given you a distinct personality with unique talents, interests, and passions. The person you are on the inside is a person worth getting to know. God already knows him perfectly. You should too.*

closing

# Takin' It to Heart

Ask your guys to finish one of the listed sentences. You may want to have them explain their answers so everyone can get to know them better.

> **You'll need—**
> • Copies of **The Next Step— Becoming a Man Who Knows Himself** (page 34), one for each student
> • Pens

- ➤ One way I'm unique is…
- ➤ One special talent, skill, or gift I have is…
- ➤ One thing I love to do is…

- ➤ One thing I'd like to change about myself is…
- ➤ The thing I like most about myself is…
- ➤ One dream I have for my future is to…

Give each guy a copy of **The Next Step— Becoming a Man Who Knows Himself** (page 34). Share an example or two of key ideas if you like. Allow some time to fill out the handouts and review their responses. Remind them to keep their papers where they can review them during the week.

End with a time of prayer. You can praise God for being unchanging and faithful, thank him for David's example, and ask for help in valuing what God values—including yourselves. If your group is small and the guys all know each other, let them pray for one another, thanking God for some specific characteristics and abilities he's given them.

Do you want to stand out? Then step down. Be a servant. If you puff yourself up, you'll get the wind knocked out of you. But if you're content to simply be yourself, your life will count for plenty.

*—Jesus, from Matthew 23, The Message*

All handouts are posted at
www.YouthSpecialties.com/free/guys
in plain text, Rich Text Format,
MS Word 95/6.0, and PDF formats.
Buyers of *Guys* can use them for *free!*

# In My Mind's Eye

businessman     teacher     missionary

nurse

photographer     administrator     musician

accountant     father

ENTREPRENEUR     FIREMAN

computer programmer     CARPENTER     disc jockey

social worker

DOCTOR     scientist

INVENTOR     PRINCIPAL     ARTIST     preacher

camp director

writer     SURVEYOR     husband

landscaper     ASTRONAUT

"The riot of discovery is a highlight of being human. You may not trek to the other side of the globe, but you can explore you and how you fit in an ever-widening world all around you. It's a frontier no one else can explore. Yes, we can give you quizzes and people can tell you what they observe, but only you can put all of the pieces together—after all, only you have any experience being you!"

—Jane Kise and Kevin Johnson in Find Your Fit (Bethany House, 1998, page 200)

"Big satisfaction comes from doing what God made you to do."

—Kevin Johnson in What Do Ya Know? (Bethany House, 2000, page 12)

# Becoming a Man Who Knows Himself

Think about the lesson we've just finished. List four or five key ideas that stand out the most.

1. _____

2. _____

3. _____

4. _____

5. _____

Which idea on your list is the most important to you? Circle it.

## Take Action

What are specific actions or steps you can take to make your circled idea a reality?

1. _____

2. _____

3. _____

# THE ISSUE

Many of today's young men have several different selves. The one who uses the locker room after practice. The one who walks the halls of school. The one who goes to work every weekend. The one who lives at home. The one who lives deep inside the soul.

But the most important self for them to identify and claim is their God-given one—a treasured son of God, wholly and dearly loved.

---

introduction
## Delvin' In

Now that your students have looked at how the world defines them and how they define themselves, it's time to look at the one true source of each person's identity—God himself. Everyone, of course, is created and loved by God equally. But for those who have chosen to be in a personal relationship with him—Christians—"created and loved by God" takes on added meaning. God's part of the equation doesn't change, as we all know. But how about the individual's part? Is an individual more important because he's a Christian? More loved? More likely to succeed? More likely to live to a ripe old age without any problems?

Hardly. The change occurs when that person realizes who he *really* is. With that realization, the person is able to call himself a child of God—and believe it. He can look forward to an eternity with Christ—even on the worst days. And he can begin brushing aside the world's false views of his worth and success.

Many, maybe even most, of your guys consider themselves to be Christians. Many, maybe even most, actually are. But do they realize the implications of that? Even many mature adults don't realize the implications. What was an obvious and simple thing to believe as a small child—"God is my daddy"—becomes increasingly difficult as a young man grows up in our pressure-filled and highly critical society.

Take some time this week to immerse yourself in Psalm 139. Read and reread the Bible verses found throughout this chapter. For you to help your students grasp their God-given identity, you must have a grasp of it yourself. Let's face it—few people regularly take the time to sit back in solitude and silence and commune with God in a father-child manner.

During this session, you'll be challenging and encouraging your guys to believe they're children of God and to live like it.

quote

"People are precious, and sometimes we forget that. They're precious because God made them."
—from Hangman's Curse by *Frank Peretti (Tommy Nelson, 2001)*

opening activity
## Warmin' Up

option [large group activity]
Getting to Know You

If you have a group of 15 or more, move any chairs out of the way and have the guys stand in the middle of the room. Explain the game to them this way—

*I'm going to call out specific descriptions, facts, or character traits of people. As soon as I do, it's your job to group up with similar people. For example, if I call out eye color, you need to find everyone who has your eye color as fast as possible. Stay in a group until I call out the next description.*

Hopefully the natural-born leaders in your group will take charge by shouting, "Size 11 shoes! Size 11 shoes! All the size 11 shoes over here on the double!"

Be sure to identify and acknowledge all the groups after each round, i.e. "Where are the January birthdays? February? March?" It's no fun to race around like a maniac if no one's going to notice.

Here's a list of characteristics for you to call out. Add your own, too.

| | |
|---|---|
| eye color | shoe size |
| birth month | number of siblings |
| year in school | introvert/extrovert |
| traffic violations— | sodas per day— |
| 0/1-3/4+ | 0/1-2/3+ |

After you've finished, ask for volunteers to name everyone in one of their groups. (Name one that had quite a few guys in it.) If you have someone who can do that, ask for another volunteer to name the people in another group. Continue until the guys can see they've remembered very little of the factual information that was made known.

option [small group activity]
Getting to Know You

If you have 14 or fewer guys, have your teens pair up. If you have an odd number, partner with one of the guys yourself. Explain the game to them this way—

*I'm going to give you one minute to find out as many vital facts about your partner as possible. You might*

*ask for birthdate, shoe size, toothbrush color, favorite movie, hero, family members, favorite school subject, and so on. When I say, "Switch," the fact-gatherer becomes the fact-giver and the fact-giver becomes the fact-gatherer. Pay attention because when the two minutes are up, we're going to see how much you can each remember about your partner.*

Live out this God-created identity the way our Father lives toward us, generously and graciously, even when we're at our worst. Our Father is kind; you be kind.

—*from Luke 6, The Message*

After the guys have finished gathering the data, ask for volunteers to share their mental lists. If competition is the grand motivator, give a prize to the team that remembers the most.

exploring the topic

# Diggin' a Little Deeper

Move into the next section with something like this—

*It's almost impossible to remember the few facts about everyone that we've covered in a short amount of time. Imagine how much more difficult it would be to remember the same details about everyone in this church, everyone in this town, everyone in this state, or everyone in the United States. Just keeping track of one minute's worth of facts on all those people would be far beyond impossible for us.*

*Think about this: God knows a complete lifetime worth of facts about every single person on the planet right now, every single person from the past, and every single person in the future. Some people might feel insignificant because of that. "I'm just one more person that God keeps catalogued in his file." But that's not true at all. The only possible reason that God would ever hold all that information in his heart would be because of how deeply he loves each and every one of us.*

Choose one or more of the following activities.

option [group activity]
## Get into Uniform

Divide your students into groups of three or four. Give each group a copy of **Get into Uniform** (page 41) and a pen. Tell the groups to designate one person to write down answers. Give your students these instructions—

**You'll need—**
- Copies of **Get into Uniform** (page 41), one for each group
- Pens
- Stopwatch
- Whiteboard and markers

*I'm going to say the name of a certain profession or individual. When I say, "Go," you'll have 45 seconds to write down as many items in the related "uniform" as possible. For example, if I say fisherman, you might write waders, fishing pole, fishing net, smelly hat with lures stuck in it, vest with big pockets, et cetera.*

*When time's up, each group will have a turn to read its list out loud. If any of the other groups have the same item, they let us know. Every group that has the same item must cross it off its list. When all the groups have finished with their lists, the group with the most remaining ideas wins.*

You can use these occupations—
- Used car salesman
- Calculus professor
- Heavy metal drummer
- College student

You'll need to decide how much leeway you'll allow in comparing answers. Is *smelly fishing hat with lures stuck in it* the same as *fishing hat*? You be the judge. When you've finished with all four rounds, make the following comments and ask some questions—

*One way we identify people is by their "uniforms." The clothing and accessories of certain occupations, teams, and clubs clearly label a person as belonging to that group. In some ways, it would be nice if there was a child-of-God uniform—not in order to draw attention to ourselves, but in order to recognize others with the same identity.*

- How would you feel about having a visible Christian "uniform" to wear?
- How do you think non-Christians view people who wear Jesus jewelry and Jesus T-shirts, use Jesus slogans, and do other Jesus things as a way to identify themselves? Explain your thinking.

quote

"It should be obvious that if a Supreme Being created me, He must love me personally. He could have created a million other people in place of me, but He chose to create me."
—Vincent P. Collins in *Me, Myself and You* (Abbey Press, 1974, page 165)

Christians don't have a visible uniform to wear, but we do have spiritual uniforms. Ephesians 6:10-18 and Colossians 3:12-17 give us two word pictures about spiritual uniforms to explore. Introduce this concept to your guys and read the passages with them. You may wish to read and discuss one passage and then the other, or you may only have time to discuss one passage. Have a volunteer record the answers to the first question for each passage on a whiteboard. Discuss these passages with questions like—

- Name the pieces of the uniform mentioned in Ephesians 6.
- What does it mean to put on the belt of truth? How do we wear it? The breastplate of righteousness? Gospel-of-peace boots? The shield of faith? The helmet of salvation? The sword of the Spirit?

- In practical, day-to-day terms, how do you act when you're wearing each of these?
- Which pieces of our uniform did you put on today? How do you know?
- Which do you wish you would have remembered to wear? Talk about that.
- Name the pieces of the uniform mentioned in Colossians 3.
- What does it mean to clothe ourselves with compassion? How do we show we're wearing it? Kindness? Humility? Gentleness? Patience? Bearing one another's burdens? Forgiveness? Thankfulness? Love?
- Which pieces of this uniform did you put on today? How do you know?
- Which do you wish you would have remembered to wear? Talk about that.
- Some might say these uniforms are the same. What do you think?

## option [video clip discussion]
### Simon Birch

Simon Birch and Joe have just been caught breaking in to the swimming coach's office. looking for clues to Joe's father's identity. Their friend, Ben, picks them up from the police station and the three of them talk about life and destiny by the lake at night. Show the clip.

**0:58:49** Ben, Joe, and Simon walk out of the police station.
**1:01:38** Joe throws a rock into the lake.

Follow up with some questions like these—

- How does the world define people like Simon? Explain your thoughts.
- Do you think people who have unique circumstances like Simon are more aware of their spiritual identities? Why or why not?
- What prevents teen girls from believing they are God's beloved children? What prevents you from believing it?

- On a scale of one (I'm a freak!) to 10 (I'm a child of God, no doubt about it!) how confident do you feel about your God-given identity? Talk about that.

## option [individual activity]
### He & Me

Give each student a copy of **He & Me** (page 42) and a pen. Explain that there are many different word pictures for the relationship between God and a Christian, for example potter and clay. In the space beside each pair of words, ask the students to write down one description of that relationship. Next to potter and clay, they might write, "molds me," "designs me with a purpose," or "views me as work of art."

When they've had a few minutes to work on this, ask some questions—

**You'll need—**
- Copies of **He & Me** (page 42) one for each student
- Pens

- Why are there so many different word pictures to describe a Christian's identity?
- Did any of the descriptions give you a negative view of your identity? If yes, do you think its possible to replace your negative view with a more positive one? Explain.
- Which description means the most to you or seems most appropriate? Talk about that.

---

Bible study
# Gettin' into the Word

**Prodigal Son**
Luke 15:11-32

**You'll need—**
- Bibles
- A robe, a ring, sandals, and other props, if you choose to act out the story (optional)

**Nudgers** (nuj´erz) *n.* a tool used to gently push teens toward new insight

- The younger son started out by knowing his identity, but not living it.
- The younger son wanted all of the "things" that went along with his identity, but didn't want any of the relationships or responsibilities.
- The younger son might have thought life with dad was a drag.
- The younger son went through a blitz of false identities-- womanizer to partier to gambler to pig-feeder to homeless to lost cause.

- When the reference point of his real identity was gone and all his false identities had fallen by the wayside, the younger son hit rock bottom.
- The younger son wasn't sure that his real identity was still available for him.
- The Father didn't merely "reinstate" the younger son. He exalted him extravagantly.
- The older son knew his identity, but he didn't seem to believe it.
- The older son thought he deserved "more" of a real identity because of his hard work.

**○ TIP**

This is a great story for students to act out. If you have a few theatrical personalities, let them do a quick, improvised rendition of this parable. If they've got creative juices, they can cast the story into several different versions—the farmer version, the big-city version, the Shakespeare version, the action-movie version.

After you've finished, move into the Bible study with a comment like this—

*It's one thing to know that God values you. It's another thing to believe it and live like it. We're going*

*to look at a story in the Bible about a young man, perhaps your age, who went through some rough times as he matured from knowing to believing to living like his father valued him.*

Assign parts and read Luke 15:11-31 as a reader's theater or have several of your students act out the story. Then use the following questions for discussion.

- Why might the younger son have decided to leave home?
- What did the younger son unknowingly give up when he rejected or ignored his identity?
- Do you think the older son had a stronger sense of identity than the younger son? Explain your thoughts.
- If Christians' real identities as God's children include acceptance, unconditional love, a sense of purpose, and a father who's always there, why do they often hide their real identities?
- What difference might there be among hiding a real identity, ignoring a real identity, and rejecting a real identity?
- Without wearing a T-shirt that says, "I am a treasured child of God," how can Christians live their true identity in practical ways?

It's in Christ that we find out who we are and what we are living for. Long before we first heard of Christ and got our hopes up, he had his eye on us, had designs on us for glorious living, part of the overall purpose he is working out in everything and everyone.
—*from Ephesians 1,* The Message

Hosea put it well: "I'll call nobodies and make them somebodies; I'll call the unloved and make them beloved. In the place where they yelled out, 'You're nobody!' they're calling you 'God's living children.'" Isaiah maintained this same emphasis:…"God doesn't count us; he calls us by name."
—*from Romans 9,* The Message

You can tell for sure that you are now fully adopted as his own children because God sent the Spirit of his Son into our lives crying out, "Papa! Father!" Doesn't that privilege of intimate conversation with God make it plain that you are not a slave, but a child? And if you are a child, you're also an heir, with complete access to the inheritance.

—*from Galatians 4, The Message*

Close the Bible study with something like this—

*According to our culture, we have to earn our way. Your value is determined solely by what you can produce, earn, or accomplish. But in the kingdom of God, you have value simply because God created you, because he loves you, because he's adopted you as his son. You can't earn his love. You can't lose it. This truth frees us from our culture's pressures to conform, produce, and accomplish to show we have value.*

*We are God's sons. That's our identity. That's our value.*

closing

# Takin' It to Heart

Give each teen a copy of **The Next Step—Becoming a Valued Son of God** (page 43). Share an example or two of key ideas if you like. Allow some time to fill out the handouts and review their responses.

**You'll need—**
- Copies of **The Next Step—Becoming a Valued Son of God** (page 43), one per teen
- Pens

Remind them to keep their papers where they can review them during the week.

End with a time of prayer in twos or threes or as a group. Here are some thoughts you might include—

*Daddy, you know how hard it is to grow up in this world. We hear so many wrong messages about how to live and who we are. Help us to not only believe we're you sons but to live that way. You've adopted us exactly as we are, to be you sons; to be part of your family; to eat, work, and play with you. Amen.*

**quote**

"You can't hide anything from God. He sees everything. And He still likes you.

—*Kevin Johnson in* What Do Ya Know? *(Bethany House, 2000, page 10)*

What marvelous love the Father has extended to us! Just look at it—we're called children of God! That's who we really are. But that's also why the world doesn't recognize us or take us seriously, because it has no idea who he is or what he's up to. But friends, that's exactly who we are: children of God.

—*from 1 John 3, The Message*

All handouts are posted at
www.YouthSpecialties.com/free/guys
in plain text, Rich Text Format,
MS Word 95/6.0, and PDF formats.
Buyers of *Guys* can use them for *free!*

When your leader calls out a profession or individual, write it in one of the spaces below. Under that make a list of items we might think of as that person's uniform. Cross out items others have on their lists and subtotal the number of items you have left in each column. Add up the subtotals for a grand total.

| profession | profession | profession | profession |
| --- | --- | --- | --- |
| | | | |
| **uniform** | **uniform** | **uniform** | **uniform** |
| | | | |
| **subtotal** | **subtotal** | **subtotal** | **subtotal** |

**total**

# HE & ME

Here is a list of biblical word pictures that illustrate your relationship with God. For each pair, write one or two ways that God interacts with you.

| HE | ME | WHAT HE DOES FOR ME |
|---|---|---|
| shepherd | sheep | He provides for me. |
| potter | clay | |
| father | son | |
| teacher | student | |
| coach | player | |
| king | subject | |
| sergeant | soldier | |
| friend | friend | |

Think about the lesson we've just finished. List four or five key ideas that stand out the most.

1. _____

2. _____

3. _____

4. _____

5. _____

Which idea on your list is the most important to you? Circle it.

### Take Action

What are specific actions or steps you can take to make your circled idea a reality?

1. _____

2. _____

3. _____

# 4 Girls
## Decoding an alien species

## ⊘ THE ISSUE

High school guys have little choice but to exist alongside high school girls, and they're not complaining about it. But it would so much easier if girls were, well, easier to understand.

---

introduction
# Delvin' In

Here we are—the "girls are just a mystery" lesson. Please note that the goal here is not to ridicule, laugh at, make fun of, or tear down those of the female sex. But it's likely that you'll have some funny comments, observations, and opinions along the way. So here's your challenge: to help your guys enjoy themselves during this lesson *without* letting them cross over the line into bad taste or offensiveness.

Let's face it. The differences between men and women are fodder for some of the funniest television shows, movies, and commercials. Who hasn't laughed at the ad featuring a posse of men hiding inside a department store clothes rack, complete with TV, snacks, and couches, while their wives do a little shopping?

Have you noticed that the male-female comparisons in ads most often poke fun at men? They're lazy. They're slobs. They're women chasers. They're beer-guzzling, football-loving, pizza-gorging, little boys who would rather play a few rounds of pool with the guys than sit down and have a heart-to-heart talk with their wives. And this image makes everyone laugh…even the guys.

But what about the women? How many of these questions sound familiar—

- ➤ Why do they talk so much?
- ➤ Why do they always go to the bathroom in herds?
- ➤ What takes them so long to get ready in the morning?

- ➤ Why does she always say, "C'mon, just talk to me. Please!"
- ➤ Why do they cry at such stupid things?
- ➤ Why can't they figure out how to change a spare tire?
- ➤ Why do they always talk about their weight?
- ➤ Why are they so sensitive?

It's all overgeneralized nonsense, isn't it?

The fact that men and women are different is a nondisputable issue. The question of whether those differences are mostly prewired or learned is a moot point. Adam and Eve had no "nurture" in the equation, only "nature," and their differences were apparent as soon as the serpent came on the scene.

As the saying goes, every rule is made to be but broken.

Lots of guys keep journals. Lots of girls are stellar athletes. Lots of guys know how to do laundry. Lots of girls drink milk straight from the carton. This lesson is not about drawing hard and fast lines in the sand. This lesson is about helping guys understand that women are wired very differently than men, by God's design, and because of that, there are some general rules that usually hold true.

This lesson isn't a manual on women. It's an invitation to appreciate the other half of God's creation.

**quote**

"I've learned that girls sweat just as much as boys."
—*age 11*

## Top Ten Ways Boys Are Different from Girls

Compiled by Linni Miller, age 4, Atlanta

1. Boys like to play with trucks more than girls.
2. Boys like to eat more than girls.
3. Boys like dinosaurs more than girls.
4. Boys are bigger than girls.
5. Boys have shorter hair than girls.
6. Boys don't wear dresses.
7. Boys don't wear their coats when it's cold outside.
8. Boys are taller than girls.
9. Boys can be daddies but girls can't.
10. Boys have tails.

## Top Ten Ways Girls Are Different from Boys

Compiled by Austen Nelson, age 4, San Diego

1. Girls wear dresses.
2. Boys wear underwear; girls wear panties.
3. Girls leave the seat down.
4. Girls have long hair.
5. Girls don't play baseball.
6. Girls don't have pee-pees.
7. Daddies have hairy bodies.
8. Girls like dolls.
9. Mommies use make-up instead of shaving cream.
10. Girls scream; boys roar.
Bonus: Girls wear fingernail polish.

*It took Linni Miller approximately five minutes to complete her list while sitting at the kitchen table neatly coloring a picture. It took Austen Nelson about four days, due to the fact that he'd previously devoted himself to a different task, namely playing with trucks, and when he finally reached number 4, he ran through the living room making engine noises and said, "Mom, can't you just do it for me?"*

---

opening activity
# Warmin' Up

### Gender Outburst

When students have arrived, read them the Top 10 lists printed in the intro.

**You'll need—**
- **The answers to Gender Outburst** (page 51), **2 copies**
- **Pen for the scorekeeper**
- **Stopwatch**

---

Then tell your guys that you're going to compile your own lists. Ask for a volunteer to be scorekeeper and a volunteer to be the emcee. Give each one a copy of the answers to **Gender Outburst** (page 51). Explain the game like this—

> **When the game begins,** [insert the emcee's name] **is going to give you a topic. You have 30 seconds to yell out as many answers as you can think of.** [Insert the scorekeeper's name] **has a list of the top five answers for each topic. When you yell a correct one, he'll mark it off on the sheet and yell, "Yes," so you know you've scored a point. Remember, think quickly and yell loudly.**

God saw all that he had made, and it was very good.
—Genesis 1:31

Let the emcee know it's his job to give the group each new topic when they're ready and to keep track of the time. Let him know how long each round will last. Tell the scorekeeper to put a checkmark by each answer the group gets right and to yell, "Yes," so they know they've scored. Play as many rounds as you have time for, but stop *before* your teens get tired of it. When play is over, ask the following questions—

- ➤ Which of your answers are true and accurate, not just stereotypes? Explain why you think so.
- ➤ How did you come up with your answers? From school? From TV? From other guys? From first-hand observation? Something else?
- ➤ What and who influences your opinions about females?
- ➤ How do your personal opinions and stereotypes about girls affect the way you think about girls? Communicate with them? Relate to them?
- ➤ Do most guys wish they understood girls better? Why or why not?

Make sure your students are clear about their lists. These are generalizations only. These are perceptions. These are opinions. Yes, there are girls who fit some of those criteria, but usually not all of them, all of the time.

exploring the topic

# Diggin' a Little Deeper

Move into the next section with an explanation like this—

> *Even though guys and girls are different, it's important not to put any more barriers between them than are already there. In fact, the goal should be to tear down some of those barriers. Don't assume that all girls are ultrasensitive just because you know one who is. Don't assume that all girls are worried about appearance more than anything else, even if it's true of some of the girls at your school. Don't assume that all girls cry over the most insignificant things, even though the girl who sits across from you in English Lit does.*
>
> *How do you feel when girls make the same broad assumptions: "All guys are slobs. All guys have only one thing on their mind. All guys are football freaks. All guys are unemotional, cold creatures who don't know a thing about women."*
>
> *Girls deserve to be understood, accepted, and appreciated for what they are—human beings quite different from you.*

Choose one or more of the following activity options.

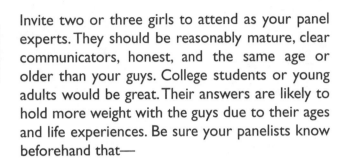

option [group activity]
## Straight from the Horse's Mouth

Invite two or three girls to attend as your panel experts. They should be reasonably mature, clear communicators, honest, and the same age or older than your guys. College students or young adults would be great. Their answers are likely to hold more weight with the guys due to their ages and life experiences. Be sure your panelists know beforehand that—

> ➤ They may get asked direct and probing questions.
> ➤ Some of the questions might be embarrassing.
> ➤ Some of the questions might seem ridiculous to them, but they should never indicate it.
> ➤ If a question hits too close to home, they have the right to pass on it.

Tell your guys that the best way to understand girls is to ask them direct questions. Trying to figure out females on their own...well, it usually doesn't work as well. Introduce your panel of experts to the group. Explain that they're here to answer whatever questions the guys may have about girls as well as they can.

Remember that guys have an image to uphold. None of them will want to appear stupid, uninformed, or immature. If no one is willing to step out and ask the first question, have a few of your own ready to get things rolling.

There are two ways to do this. First, let the guys raise their hands and ask questions directly. If you think your group is confident enough to do this, it's an efficient way to go. A second way is to let the guys write single questions on pieces of paper anonymously. Then the panel reads and answers the questions one by one. This may encourage your guys to ask questions they might be too embarrassed to ask otherwise, and it may help your panel feel less on-the-spot, especially if they know some of the guys personally.

The Lord God said, "It is not good for the man to be alone. I will make a helper suitable for him."

*—Genesis 2:18*

You need to act as emcee for the activity in the following ways—

> ➤ If a question is clearly inappropriate, simply say, "We'll pass on that one," without embarrassing the questioner.
> ➤ If your panelists tend to be long-winded, help them keep their answers to a reasonable length by turning to another panelist and asking for her thoughts.
> ➤ If guys are hesitating to ask questions, get the discussion moving by asking some questions of your own. Be prepared so there are no long, awkward silences. Here are some ideas—

—It seems like girls are more moody once a month. Is that just our imagination, or are those few days really more difficult for you?

—Why don't girls just come out and say what they really mean? Like, "I hate that restaurant" instead of, "Are you sure you want to eat there?"

—Can guys and girls be good friends without being romantically involved?

option [video clip discussion]
**Grease**

Show two scenes from *Grease*. The first scene shows the summer romance between Danny (John Travolta) and Sandy (Olivia Newton-John).

This sets up the second scene, in which Danny and Sandy relate tales of their summer romance—in completely different ways.

**0:00:00** The opening scene of *Grease*.
**0:01:25** The summer romance scene fades.

**0:13:50** The guys on the bleachers ask Danny about his summer romance.
**0:17:48** The song ends with the phrase, "Tell me more."

Ask the following questions—

> ➤ What were the girls interested in hearing about from Sandy?
> ➤ What were the guys interested in hearing about from Danny?
> ➤ Do you think Sandy was relating events as she really experienced them or as she wanted her friends to think they happened? What about Danny? Why do you think so?
> ➤ How can two people view the exact same event in two totally different ways?
> ➤ Have you ever been in a situation where guys and girls had entirely different opinions, ideas, perspectives, and observations? Talk about that.

option [individual activity]
Understand Her,
Understand Her Not

Give each student a copy of **Understand Her, Understand Her Not** (page 52) and a pen. Let them work on it for several

**You'll need—**

• Copies of **Understand Her, Understand Her Not** (page 52), one for each student
• Pens

minutes. Regather and ask for volunteers to share and explain their answers. Then ask some questions—

> ➤ What do you think girls don't understand about guys?
> ➤ Why do you think God made men and women—whom he intended to be life partners—so different?

- Do you find yourself being annoyed by, confused about, indifferent to, or genuinely interested in the girls in your life? Why?
- If you could change one thing about the way guys and girls relate to each other, what would it be? Explain your thinking.

> Wise men and women are always learning, always listening for fresh insights.
>
> —from Proverbs 18, The Message

Bible study

# Gettin' into the Word

## Jesus and Women
Selected Verses

After you've finished the Diggin' a Little Deeper activities, say something like this—

**You'll need—**
- 3 copies of **Jesus and Women**, (page 53)
- **Bibles**
- **Pens**

**Nudgers** (nuj´erz) *n.* a tool used to gently push teens toward new insight

- Jesus never treated women as second class citizens or as property.
- When it was time to feed the 5,000, Jesus didn't coordinate a women's potluck committee. He put the men to work.
- Jesus commanded men to respect their wives more than the law commanded: don't even *think* about another woman adulterously; don't assume that granting your wife a legal certificate of divorce will make everything a-okay.
- Jesus defined true religion as, among other things, caring for the widows.

- Jesus treated even corrupt (adulterous) and "unclean" (hemorrhaging) women with the utmost respect and decency.
- When other men sneered at the woman caught in adultery, Jesus did not. He was thoughtful enough to take the focus off her humiliation and redirect it to the sand where he wrote.
- While Jesus suffered on the cross, the women stayed with him.
- When Jesus was in the grave, it was women who went first to anoint and care for his body.

*All you have to do is spend five minutes in the hallway of any school, from kindergarten to college, to know for sure that guys and girls are different. It's no big revelation. God designed us differently. It was his intent all along that the differences would complement one another. But often they end up doing just the opposite—pitting men against women, males against females, guys against girls.*

*Trying to understand the differences between men and women is a good start. But that's all it is—a start. The next step is the most important one—learning to value the differences, learning to view the differences as a good thing, and learning to treat women with the respect and honor they deserve.*

**quote**

"I've learned that I don't understand women, and I never will."
—age 84

Divide your students into three groups. Give each group a copy of **Jesus and Women** (page 53). Make sure Bibles are available for everyone. Assign each group to read one of the following stories—

- Jesus and the bleeding woman (Luke 8:43-48)
- Jesus and the woman caught in adultery (John 8:1-11)
- Jesus' feet anointed (Mark 14:1-9)

After the group reads its story, the group members should work together to answer the questions on the handout. After they've finished, gather the three groups together. Ask a person from each group to read their story to the entire group. When all three stories have been read, review their answers. Then ask application questions like these—

- *Compare the way that Jesus treated women with the way the media and our society treat women.*
- *Give examples of how women are portrayed in movies and music and on television, how men are portrayed, and how men treat women. Which of these examples should you follow and which should you avoid?*
- *What kind of female students in your school receive the most respect from guys? The least?*
- *Explain why the respect men give to women shouldn't be influenced by the "the kind of women" they are. (Think about Jesus' example.)*
- *What changes do you need to make in the way you view or treat the women in your life?*

End the lesson with a few comments—

*Relating to gals can be confusing for young men today, but if we commit ourselves to be like Jesus, we commit ourselves to treating women like Jesus would—*

- Jesus treated women the same way he treated men, with respect and honor.
- God made women different from men. The differences aren't a mistake. They're part of God's plan.
- We need each other. God created it that way.
- Women are given gifts and talents just like men, and God expects women to use them. If he doesn't want us burying our talents, he doesn't want us to bury someone else's talents, either.

- Most women are attracted to men who treat them like Jesus treated them. Women love men who love Jesus and who treat women with respect and honor. Being strong enough to treat a woman with respect is being strong enough to be a man of God.

closing
# Takin' It to Heart

Give everyone a copy of **The Next Step—Becoming a Man Who Respects Women** (page 54). Share an

**You'll need—**
- Copies of **The Next Step— Becoming a Man Who Respects Women** (page 54)

example or two of key ideas if you like. Allow some time to fill out the handouts and review their responses. Remind them to keep their papers where they can review them during the week.

Close in prayer, perhaps leading your students in a time of silent confession. You may also use this prayer

*Dear God,*
*We need your help to understand women—all the women in our lives, mothers, sisters, friends, girlfriends, teachers, coworkers. Help us to show respect and honor toward all the women in our lives, to encourage them, to bless them, to love them. Use our time today to make us more like Jesus. Amen*

All handouts are posted at
www.YouthSpecialties.com/free/guys
in plain text, Rich Text Format,
MS Word 95/6.0, and PDF formats.
Buyers of *Guys* can use them for *free!*

# GENDER OUTBURST

Give one copy of this sheet to the emcee to announce the topics and one copy to the scorekeeper to check off the correct answers.

**1. Things some girls do when getting ready for school**

- ❑ wash their hair
- ❑ curl their eyelashes
- ❑ pluck their eyebrows
- ❑ floss their teeth
- ❑ try on seven outfits before choosing one

**2. Things some girls do in their spare time**

- ❑ go to the indoor mall
- ❑ go to the strip mall
- ❑ go to the discount mall
- ❑ go to the on-line mall
- ❑ shop

**3. Things some girls can't do**

- ❑ take a joke
- ❑ be quiet
- ❑ pull a piece of spaghetti through their noses and out their mouths
- ❑ drink a two-liter bottle of Mountain Dew in one sitting
- ❑ change the oil in their cars

**4. Weird things some girls do**

- ❑ skip the Wimbledon championship match
- ❑ skip the Stanley Cup playoffs
- ❑ skip the NBA championship game
- ❑ skip the Super Bowl
- ❑ skip the World Series

**5. Things guys don't understand about girls**

- ❑ why they go to the bathroom in groups
- ❑ why they carry a purse
- ❑ why they cry during Kodak commercials
- ❑ why they like to watch Olympic figure skating
- ❑ why they always worry about their hair

**6. The scariest things girls say to guys**

- ❑ Can we just talk about it?
- ❑ Wanna go shopping?
- ❑ Let's just be good friends.
- ❑ What do you think of my haircut?
- ❑ Hey, didn't I see you renting *Titanic* last night?

**7. Worst compliments girls can give guys**

- ❑ Gee, that haircut really brings out your cheekbones.
- ❑ Great sweater. Can I borrow it sometime?
- ❑ You'd be a perfect Munchkin for the school play.
- ❑ Wow, when I wear these platforms I'm taller than you.
- ❑ Can you teach me how to make my voice change sounds like that?

# Understand Her,
# Understand Her Not

In the first column, write the name of the female you understand the most. It can be your mom or a friend, cousin, sibling, classmate. Whoever. Write reasons why you understand her.

In the second column, write the name of a female you don't understand and give reasons why you don't understand her.

**The female I understand the most**

**Reasons**

**The female I understand the least**

**Reasons**

# JESUS and WOMEN

Mark the passage your leader assigns to you for study.

- ☐ Jesus and the bleeding woman *Luke 8:43-48*
- ☐ Jesus and the woman caught in adultery *John 8:1-11*
- ☐ Jesus' feet anointed *Mark 14:1-9*

## Life for Women during Bible Times

✔ Women were treated like property, indicating the status or position of their husbands.

✔ Men could have multiple wives. Women were allowed only one husband.

✔ Adultery was generally considered a crime, committed against husbands only.

✔ Greek and Roman men were allowed to kill their wives if they appeared in public without veils.

✔ Widowed women were at the mercy of sons or other family members for financial support; otherwise they resorted to begging, prostitution, and illegal activity.

✔ Women were considered uneducable and unreliable as courtroom witnesses.

✔ Because newborn girls had little value in society's eyes, they were often discarded after birth, put outside where anyone could take them. They usually died or were raised to be slaves or prostitutes.

✔ The Pharisees commonly prayed, "Thank you, God, that I am not a slave, a Gentile, or a woman."

After reading the passage, discuss the following in your group—

✔ Describe the woman from the viewpoint of someone who was there (other than Jesus).

✔ What do you suppose people thought of the woman based on the way they spoke to her and treated her in this passage?

✔ What was Jesus' opinion of the woman, based on the way he treated her?

✔ What risks did Jesus take in treating the woman as he did?

Think about the lesson we've just finished. List four or five key ideas that stand out the most.

1. _____

2. _____

3. _____

4. _____

5. _____

Which idea on your list is the most important to you? Circle it.

## Take Action

What are specific actions or steps you can take to make your circled idea a reality?

1. _____

2. _____

3. _____

# Dating and Sexuality
Everything you've ever wanted to know that can fit into one session

## 🔵 THE ISSUE

For many teens, the subjects of sexuality and dating are in-your-face topics. Unfortunately, they're getting most of their information from the entertainment industry and their peers. It's time to reverse that trend and show teens that the church is ready to talk about these two issues in a biblically truthful and culturally relevant way.

---

introduction
## Delvin' In

At last. The lesson we all (or at least most of your guys) have been waiting for. And for good reason. The attraction they feel for the opposite sex is natural, God-designed, and good. But the attraction isn't the issue. The *actions* based on that attraction is the heart of the matter.

The reasons dating and sexuality are included in this book is simple—they're issues that both guys and girls want to discuss, the topics are vital elements of their identity, and they're perfect topics to address in guys-only, girls-only settings.

### 🎯 TIP

If you're working with older teens and you and your guys want to pursue this topic in more detail, check out *Good Sex: A Whole-Person Approach to Teenage Sexuality & God* by Jim Hancock and Kara Eckmann Powell (Youth Specialties, 2001).

That's not to say that guys and girls can't handle talking about this issue together. They can. They do. Go ahead and ask them. But maybe guys and girls need a structured forum for discussing these issues with their own gender. Besides, there are better options for a guy's discussion than the locker room.

Your group with this curriculum is one of those better options.

*Fact:* they're at (or very near) a sexually mature age. *Fact:* their testosterone levels are skyrocketing. *Fact:* thanks to technology and the media, the world is a visual playground, and guys are visually aroused. No one should try to tell your students that those feelings and physical reactions are wrong. In fact, they're right. They're God-given.

But parents, ministers, and youth leaders are right, too—regardless of the sexual maturity, the hormone levels, or the abundance of visual stimulation, sexual activity is to be reserved for marriage. These messages are more than a minor conflict. A major head-on collision is waiting to happen. Wham!

No one can change the physical urges of teen guys. Nor can anyone change the cultural trend toward older and older newlyweds. Sure, 75 or 100 years ago, most of your guys would be living in a marital relationship that coincided with their physical maturity. But this is the 21st century. Marriage comes later, hormones come when they want, the world says, "Have safe sex," and the church says, "Have no sex at all until you've said, 'I do.'"

What a rotten predicament.

There are two main philosophies in the Christian culture about dating. The first is to give up the institution of dating completely, as outlined in the best-selling book *I Kissed Dating Goodbye*. The second is to actively participate in the dating world, but only within God's principles. *Boundaries in Dating* is just one of the many books available that lay out this second philosophy.

Unfortunately, God doesn't lay out any hard-and-fast dating rules in the Bible. There are many clear instructions on sex and marriage, but nothing even remotely related to "Thou shalt not stay out past the hour of 11 p.m." Neither are there ideas for super dates, how to carry on a conversation, what to wear, or where to eat.

This lesson will take a very small but very determined stab at helping to lay a foundation. Rest assured, if you handle it right, there won't be any awkward moments of silence. This is one topic that keeps things lively.

## ⊙ TIP

**You may want to copy and mail the parent letter found on page 67. (Or adapt it to your situation.) Give parents an opportunity to call you with suggestions or concerns.**

### quote

*"I've learned that a teenager's biggest fear is the fear of a broken heart."*

—age 16

## opening activity
# Warmin' Up

**Whose Dating Line Is It Anyway?**

This activity will be great fun *if* you gear it to your specific group. If you have a lot of introverts, let them set the pace and the tone of the game. Don't push them too far, and don't force them into working either alone or in a pair. Let them choose which they prefer. If you have a lot of extroverts, sit back and enjoy the entertainment.

### You'll need—

- 1 copy of **Whose Dating Line Is It Anyway?** (page 61)
- Props such as a telephone, a steering wheel, a football jersey or letterman jacket, pom-poms, studious-looking glasses, textbooks, plastic or silk flowers

Use the scenarios on **Whose Dating Line Is It Anyway?** (page 61). For each scenario, there is an example you can give to jumpstart your students' thinking.

Explain the game to your students—

*I'll describe a situation. It's your job to come up with a word, phrase, or sentence that fits. For example, if the card says, "Worst thing a girl can say when you ask what she wants to do on a date" you could give the following lines—*

- ➤ *"I don't know. What do you want to do?"*
- ➤ *"A date? I never said I'd go on a date with you!"*

*I'll call out one or more names. You'll come up, pick a prop if you'd like, and deliver your line. There aren't right or wrong lines. Just have fun and be creative.*

Call on several students to perform for each card. It usually takes at least one or two students to get the enthusiasm rolling. Keep things moving quickly. No lag time allowed.

Use the samples to jump-start the thinking of your less dramatic guys. When you're done, vote on the funniest, the most likely to actually happen, the least likely to actually happen, and the most original.

## exploring the topic
# Diggin' a Little Deeper

Move into the next section with comments like—

*It's easy—and pretty hilarious—to imagine all the embarrassing and funny things that might happen on a date...until one of them actually happens. This thing called the Dating Game isn't really a game at all. It's serious stuff.*

The Lord God said, "It is not good for the man to be alone."

—Genesis 2:18

Choose one or more of the following activities.

- ➤ What might God think about dating? Why do you think that?
- ➤ Can you think of any stories from the Bible that might relate to the issue of dating? What are they?
- ➤ Is it okay for a Christian to go on a date with a non-Christian? Why or why not?
- ➤ What are your parents' guidelines for dating? What do you think about them?
- ➤ If you asked out a girl and then found out her father expected to meet you first, what would do? Why?

## option [group activity]
## National Weather Brainstorm Warning

Before you begin, make two columns on the whiteboard. Title one DATING PROS, and the second one DATING CONS.

**You'll need—**
- Whiteboard
- Markers

Ask for a volunteer to be the whiteboard CEO and write down key words of the brainstorming ideas.

Explain to your group that there are many different ways to view dating. Begin with the Dating Pros and ask for ideas about the positive aspects of dating. For example, "A chance to talk about things," or "A way to get to know another person better."

After you have a list of positive ideas, move to Dating Cons. An example of this is, "It can put people in awkward and tempting situations." Push your guys to think beyond the simple answers. The cons of dating may present real-life issues for at least some of your guys (though you don't have to make them admit it).

Now's your chance to provide some positive input that can counter all the ridiculous ideas about dating that are floating around in magazines and on TV. After finishing the two lists, ask your guys to brainstorm ideas for creative dates. You don't have to write these down, though you may want to keep a record of them for your own files. When you've finished, ask the following questions or some of your own—

## option [video activity]
## Back in the Saddle Again

Sam (Tom Hanks) has been a widower for about a year. Show the scene in which Sam finally gets up the nerve to get "back in the saddle again" and ask out a woman.

**You'll need—**
- *Sleepless in Seattle*
- TV and VCR

**0:42:45** Right after Tom walks down the stairs and the music starts.
**0:44:30** Tom sits down and the music ends.

Ask questions like these or some of your own—

- ➤ What's so scary about asking out a girl? How can we avoid or ease our fears?

- What's the hardest way to ask out a girl? The easiest?
- If a girl were here, what would she say is the nicest way to be asked out?
- How do you feel about girls asking out guys?

option [individual activity]
*Date Sale*

Hand out a copy of **Date Sale** (page 62) and a pen to each guy. Go over the directions on the top of the sheet with them. Give them several minutes to make their picks. Regroup and ask each guy (if you have time, otherwise ask for volunteers) to read his finished list. Then ask questions—

> **You'll need—**
> - Copies of **Date Sale** (page 62), one for each guy
> - Pens

- What did you base your choices on?
- In what ways was this shopping spree like real life?
- What is the one most important thing for you in deciding whether you want to ask a girl out? Explain.

Bible study
# Gettin' into the Word

**The Spirit of the Law**
Selected verses

> **You'll need—**
> - Copies of **Heart and Soul** (page 63), one for each guy
> - Copies of **Plan for Peace in Your Dating Life** (pages 64-65), one for each guy
> - Pens
> - Bibles

Move into the Bible study with something like this—

*Most teenagers have a lot of questions about dating and sexuality. Teens who aren't believers probably get most of their information, guidelines, and instruction from the media—TV, magazines, and movies. But where can a Christian—knowing that the media's message isn't entirely true or accurate—go for answers? The Bible leaves a lot of blanks in terms of dating and sexuality. The Bible makes two principles exceedingly clear—*

> *People who are dating must respect one another in every possible way.*
> *Sexual intercourse before marriage is a sin.*

*But that leaves a lot to figure out, doesn't it? We're going to look at a few verses in the Bible to see if we can't come up with some guidelines for healthy sexuality and dating. Then*

> How beautiful you are, my darling! Oh, how beautiful! Your eyes are doves.
>
> —Song of Songs 1:15

*we'll look at some great advice from a guy who knows what's going on with dating, sexuality, and teenagers.*

Hand out **Heart and Soul** (page 63) and pens to all the guys. Work on this activity as a group. It's a great opportunity for you to listen to your students' insights, concerns, fears, questions, and confusion about dating and sexuality.

**⊙ TIP**
This topic will be addressed again from a different viewpoint in the next session, "Blessed Are the Pure in Heart."

Have one student read the first set of verses listed on the handout. If other translations are available, let your students read from those also.

Facilitate honest and open discussion with the following questions and others of your own. Be confident. This *is* a topic they want to talk about.

- ➤ How does God want you to view your body?
- ➤ What messages do you get from the media about how to view your body?
- ➤ Why do you think talking about sex, reading about sex, watching movies about sex, and actually participating in sex are so prevalent among high schoolers?
- ➤ What might change that trend?
- ➤ What do you think prevents so many people from treating their bodies with dignity?

Ask another student to read the second passage of Scripture. Read it from other translations you might have. Discuss questions like the following—

- ➤ These verses say we should concentrate on pleasing God. Who do you think teens in general try to please the most? Talk about that. Who do you—honestly—try to please the most? Talk about that.
- ➤ Pleasing God isn't supposed to be a dreadful event. As Paul writes in *The Message,* it's supposed to be a "living, spirited dance." What does that mean? How can you pursue that?
- ➤ What's your parents' definition of sexual promiscuity? Your church's definition? Your friends' definitions? Yours?
- ➤ God describes humans as being both body and soul, both mind and spirit. We aren't made of only physical or emotional or intellectual parts, but rather all three. What implications does that have for people who have sex before being married? Explain your thinking. Will both guys and girls be affected the same way?
- ➤ What can you do to prevent yourself from engaging in sexually promiscuous activity? (It won't happen by itself. You must have a plan.)

After discussing these questions, hand out **Plan for Peace in Your Dating Life** (pages 64-65) to each guy, and work through it as a group.

After you and your teens have talked through the handout, ask a few closing questions—

- ➤ We've had some good discussion on the topics of dating and girls. What have you found to be most helpful? Least helpful?
- ➤ What do you want to be different because of this session?
- ➤ What might you need to help make those changes a reality?

Close with comments like—

*Most non-Christians and many Christians think it's crazy of God to ask adolescents to keep their clothes on until they get married. Most would say it's unrealistic to ask a young man not to have sex until he's married…after all, everyone's doing it. Well the truth is not everyone else is doing it. A bunch of kids are working hard to keep their sexual life pure. Let me share some thoughts with you that may help you as you make important decisions about your body and about when and whom you're going to share it with.*

- ➤ *God designed men to get physically aroused, but our culture has the distorted that truth into, "It's unnatural to even try to control your desires or body."*
- ➤ *The truth is you can learn to control your thoughts and your actions. It takes commitment, accountability, and practice.*
- ➤ *The best way to prepare for a healthy marriage is to keep yourself sexually pure before marriage.*

The information contained in **Plan for Peace in Your Dating Life** is taken from *Sex & Dating: Let's Talk About It,* a video seminar by Mike and Eva Ashburn. Mike Ashburn also has presented this seminar to thousands of teens across the country. It's biblically sound, culturally relevant, and dignified. To order the video or to book a live appearance contact Gospel Seed Productions, P.O. Box 546, Fishers, IN 46038, 800/341-9902.

> - *The quickest way to kill any relationship is to become sexually involved outside of marriage.*
> - *The back-seat of a car is not the place to be setting your boundaries. Do it now, and commit yourself to sticking to them.*
> - *Prayer, the Holy Spirit, and God's power are real. Use 'em!*

closing

# Takin' It to Heart

Give each guy a copy of **The Next Step— Becoming a Man Who Sets Sexual Boundaries** (page 66). Share an example or two of key points if you like. Allow some time to fill out the handouts and review their responses. Remind them to keep their papers where they can review them during the week.

End with a time of prayer.

*Lord, you know how hard it is to grow up in this world. And we hear lies so often they begin to seem like truth. Help us to have integrity in our dating lives, to rely on your strength during temptations, and to change our desires into your desires. Use this time to help change our lives. Thanks, Lord, for being our faithful and all-powerful God. Amen.*

**You'll need—**
- Copies of **The Next Step— Becoming a Man Who Sets Sexual Boundaries** (page 66), one for each student
- Pens

Jacob was in love with Rachel and said [to her father], "I'll work for you seven years in return for your younger daughter Rachel." So Jacob served seven years to get Rachel, but they seemed like only a few days to him because of his love for her.

—*Genesis 29:18, 20*

**quote**

"Ideally, a Christian [approach to dating] means seeing a person as *a person*, rather than as an object to be won through persistence or through clever study or even as a potential mate right off the bat. It means seeing that person as belonging to *God*."

—*from* Dating: Clues for the Clueless *(Promise Press, 1999)*

All handouts are posted at
www.YouthSpecialties.com/free/guys
in plain text, Rich Text Format,
MS Word 95/6.0, and PDF formats.
Buyers of *Guys* can use them for *free!*

# Who's Dating Line Is It Anyway?

**Worst turndown line a girl can give you**

I've got to groom my poodle that night.

**Worst ask-out line from a girl**

Will you go to prom with me and don't say no or I'll cry.

**Worst conversation starter by a guy**

Do you always paint your nails such a pukey color?

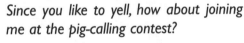

**Worst conversation starter by a girl**

So, it looks like you've finally started to shave.

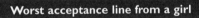

**Worst way for a guy to ask out a cheerleader**

Since you like to yell, how about joining me at the pig-calling contest?

**Worst acceptance line from a girl**

Sure, I'll go the movies with you. I've got nothing better going on, and since it's dark in the theater, I won't have to look at you.

**Worst thing your dad could say to your date**

Make sure Steven gets you home early. He needs his rest, too, you know.

**Worst thing your date's dad could say to you**

I was checking on your driving record, and I've got a question or two.

**Worst thing to say when your date asks if you brought flowers**

Flowers? Flowers? What kind of idiot would want flowers?

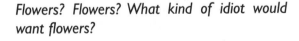

**Worst way to be asked to a movie**

Since every other guy said no, how about watching The Parent Trap with me?

**Dating and Sexuality** | 61

Check out these date traits, then buy $47 worth of the ones you most want in a girl you date. Place a check in the box beside your choices. Your total bill must be exactly $47 dollars (not one dollar more or less).

**DATE SALE**

## $10 Traits

- ❑ smart
- ❑ Christian
- ❑ honest
- ❑ good sense of humor
- ❑ easy to talk to
- ❑ good looking
- ❑ student leader in her youth group
- ❑ not overly talkative
- ❑ your choice, not listed on this page

## $5 Traits

- ❑ nice to everyone at school
- ❑ athletic
- ❑ willing to go Dutch
- ❑ teaches Sunday School
- ❑ musically talented
- ❑ has nice parents
- ❑ smiles a lot

## $1 Traits

- ❑ shorter than you
- ❑ Homecoming queen
- ❑ attends same church
- ❑ has nice friends
- ❑ has same hobbies
- ❑ likes to watch football

Not too easy, was it? Now pretend that money is no object. It doesn't matter what your bill totals. Pick your top 10 favorite traits by circling them.

Just because something is technically legal doesn't mean that it's spiritually appropriate. If I went around doing whatever I thought I could get by with, I'd be a slave to my whims.

You know the old saying, "First you eat to live, and then you live to eat"? Well, it may be true that the body is only a temporary thing, but that's no excuse for stuffing your body with food, or indulging it with sex. Since the Master honors you with a body, honor him with your body! Remember that your bodies are created with the same dignity as the Master's body.

—*I Corinthians 6 (verses 12-15)* The Message

One final word, friends. We ask you—*urge* is more like it—that you keep on doing what we told you to do to please God, not in a dogged religious plod, but in a living, spirited dance. You know the guidelines we laid out for you from the Master Jesus. God wants you to live a pure life.

Keep yourselves from sexual promiscuity.

—*I Thessalonians 4 (verses 1-3)* The Message

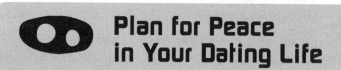

# Plan for Peace in Your Dating Life

## In General...

**Girls are led by their emotions and their hearts. Guys are led by their eyes and their imaginations.**

*What implications does that have for you in dating? In school? In physical movement?*

**According to some people, guys give love to get sex, and girls give sex to get love.**

*In what ways do you see these statements as true? As false?*

*Let's say, for the sake of discussion, that the statements are true. How does this make the guy feel? The girl? Explain your answer.*

*What do you think about guys who try to coax, trick, or force girls into having sexual intercourse by using the if-you-loved-me-you'd-have-sex-with-me tactic?*

---

For as high as the heavens are above the earth, so great is his love for those who fear him; as far as the east is from the west, so far has he removed our transgressions from us.

—Psalm 103:12 NIV

If we confess our sins, he is faithful and just and will forgive us our sins and purify us from all unrighteousness.

—1 John 1:9 NIV

Though your sins are like scarlet, they shall be as white as snow; though they are red as crimson, they shall be like wool.

—Isaiah 1:18 NIV

---

**If someone has had sexual intercourse before marriage and he or she asks God for forgiveness, God delivers on his promise. In God's eyes, that person is pure.**

*Do you believe the last statement is true? Why or why not?*

*Do a guy and girl who've had premarital sex together experience the same amount of guilt? Why do you think that?*

*If God now sees the person as pure, does that mean the person won't experience any effects from the sexual experience? Explain your answer.*

*Where might there be different standards for guys and girls in terms of their virginity? For example, women should be virgins when they marry, but guys don't need to be. Talk about this.*

---

The ideas in Plan for Peace in Your Dating Life are adapted from the video *Dating and Sexuality: Let's Talk about It* by Mike and Eva Ashburn (Gospel Seed Productions, 1997.) Used with permission. All rights reserved.

# Think About It

## Don't play mind games with each other.
*What do you think this statement means?*

*Are guys or girls more likely to play mind games? Or do both sexes play mind games, only in different ways? Talk about that. What's wrong with playing mind games?*

## Guys should ask out girls face to face.
*Do you agree with this statement? Why or why not?*

*Is face-to-face rejection more painful than over-the-phone rejection? Explain your thinking.*

## When a guy asks out a girl, there are only two possible answers—yes or no.
*Would you rather be turned down with a clear no or with an ease-the-pain excuse?*

# The Only Dating Guideline You'll Ever Need

*Limit yourself to kissing, hugging, and holding hands...and that may be too much for some.*

## Why only kissing, hugging, and holding hands?
*Because most of the trouble starts after that.*

## When might kissing, hugging, and holding hands be too much?
*When it makes a guy or girl want more than just that.*

*When it makes a guy or girl imagine impure thoughts.*

*(And if the previous two results are true for you, you should examine more closely your kissing, hugging, and holding hands.)*

## When you're thinking about kissing a girl you don't know very well, ask yourself these questions—
*What's my reason for kissing her? (Think about what your kiss communicates to her.)*

*Am I treating her in a way that's consistent with biblical principles—to respect others and act in their best interests?*

Think about the lesson we've just finished. List four or five key ideas that stand out the most.

1. _____

2. _____

3. _____

4. _____

5. _____

Which idea on your list is the most important to you? Circle it.

## Take Action

What are specific actions or steps you can take to make your circled idea a reality?

1. _____

2. _____

3. _____

# Sample Parent Letter

On Wednesday evenings we're working through Girls: 10 Gutsy, God-Centered Sessions on Issues That Matter to Girls and Guys: 10 Fearless, Faith-Focused Sessions on Issues That Matter to Guys. The guys and girls are meeting in separate groups during this time so that they're better able to discuss issues that are relevant to them. While guys and girls are concerned with many of the same issues—friends, parents, future plans, emotions—this curriculum helps them approach the subjects from their unique viewpoints.

In a few weeks, we will be tackling the issue of dating and sexuality. Certainly the world's view of dating and sexuality is anything but God-centered, so it's a challenging topic. We want to reassure you that, though we will be encouraging very open and honest discussion and though we will welcome any questions your daughter or son may have, we are committed to—

- presenting biblical truths
- steering students toward a godly view of dating
- honoring your sacred role as parents

If you have any questions, or if you would like to see the lessons we'll be using, please call me at the church office.

Thank you for the privilege of being a small part of your child's journey toward a deeper and more mature faith.

In His Grip,

*Hershel Berzacky*

Youth Director

# 6

# Blessed Are the Pure in Heart...
## For they will see God

## ⊘ THE ISSUE

True love waits. It's all over the teenage Christian media. It's the only way to be pure in God's sight. But Jesus was just as interested in following the spirit of the law as he was in following the letter of the law, which means minds must be as pure as bodies. Therein lies the challenge, perhaps the greatest challenge we face—to make the insides of our lives and the outsides of our lives reflect the heart of Christ! The battle is in the mind.

### introduction
## Delvin' In

In our culture of glorified sex, it's a big challenge for anyone—especially teen guys who are at the peak of their sexual maturity—to live a physically pure life. They're encouraged to demonstrate their manhood by having sex with the hottest girls they can entice. That first sexual experience is a rite of passage from boyhood into manhood in many cultures. But not in ours. It carries no such significance. It's just another way to experience immediate gratification.

But there's more to it than just needing to conquer immediate gratification. Sex has always been the great unknown to those who are uninitiated. For all young people, sex is a fascinating topic. It is an unknown, a mystery. They want to know about a part of life that has been unknown to them until now.

Hopefully, the Christian guys in your youth group have already rejected the world's message about the importance of sexual prowess, but that doesn't make it any easier to remain physically pure. Even if they do manage to protect their physical purity, protecting their hearts' and minds' purity is another matter entirely.

Guys are aroused by what they see and what they imagine. Their eyes and their brains are their two worst enemies. That doesn't bode well in this society of suggestive billboards, scantily clothed models, a wild-frontier Internet, and sexually laced athletic events. Let's face it. Sex sells. And the most eager buyers are men. Nearly naked women will affect men much more quickly and decisively than nearly naked men will affect women (which is not to say that women aren't affected by what they see—they are, but not at the same lightning speed.)

It's *natural* to think about sex. It's *okay* to think about sex. If more people thought about it rationally there might not be so much irrational behavior. But it is *not okay* to imagine oneself having sexual intercourse outside of marriage. Jesus challenges us to follow the spirit of the law, not just the letter of the law. The letter of the law says, "Don't engage in sex before marriage." The spirit of the law says, "Don't *imagine* engaging in sex before marriage."

Those are some fightin' words, and the battle lines have been drawn. Thankfully we've got God fighting alongside us, not against us.

### opening activity
## Warmin' Up

**And the Winner Is . . .**

Divide your students into groups of three or four. Hand out pens and copies of **And the Winner Is . . .** (page 74) to each group. This is a small-scale People's Choice Awards activity. Tell the guys they must come to an agreement on every answer. Give them seven to 10 minutes to finish.

> **You'll need—**
> • Copies of **And the Winner Is . . .** (page 74), one for each group
> • Pens

Then gather everyone together and ask the following questions—

> ➤ List three or four elements that are in almost every one of your favorite movies (sex, suspense, action, comedy, manhunt).
> ➤ List three or four elements that are in almost every one of your favorite TV shows. (Most sex on television is still by innuendo, but don't let your students ignore it simply because it's not as blatant as it is in movies.)
> ➤ When you see a beautiful, sexy woman on the screen, how does it affect you?
> ➤ When you see either real or implied sexual activity on the screen, how does it affect you?
> ➤ Is it possible for a guy to see those images and completely ignore them? What should you do?

**quote**

"Movies, videos, music, pornography, day-dreaming, dating without boundaries, casual kisses that aren't so casual—all these things add to the pressure you feel."
—*Kevin Johnson in* What Do Ya Know *(Bethany House, 2000)*

exploring the topic

# Diggin' a Little Deeper

Say something like this before you move into the next activity—

> *When a guy sees a suggestive image, his body almost always unconsciously engages, even if his brain and heart don't. Truthfully, many guys can't stop their bodies from getting sexually revved up when they're just entering puberty. This can be very awkward and scary when they're caught off guard by their own arousal. Soon enough though, every guy begins to know that he can control the natural sexual arousal of his body.*
>
> *The real problem that needs to be addressed is intentional sexual thoughts. Most guys say, "Hey, I can't*

*help what I'm thinking about. It's out of my control." But is that really true, or is that just an easy way out? Instead of simply writing off impure thoughts as out of our control or normal, let's look at some active steps to live with the sexual integrity God desires.*

Choose one or more of the following activities.

option [group activity]
## Is God Cool with This?

Divide your guys into several groups and hand out **Is God Cool with This?** (page 75) and pens. As a group, they need to

**You'll need—**
- Copies of **Is God Cool with This?** (page 75), one for each group
- Pens

decide whether God is cool with the activity, he's not cool with it, or something in between. They should be able to defend their answers. When you regather, give each group an opportunity to share one of its answers and explain it. Continue through the handout.

Through this activity, help your guys talk about the issues involved with living in the world carefully and wisely (as opposed to living a completely sheltered life except for church, youth group, and a Christian concert).

option [group video activity]
## Where Have All the Movies Gone?

One of the goals for this session is to help students recognize that what they see can have a measurable effect on their thoughts and actions. It's next to impossible to find current movies containing scenes that promote—or demonstrate—physical and personal purity. So you'll have to pursue this discussion without a corresponding video clip.

You might want to introduce these questions with somthing like this—

*I wanted to show you a video clip that showed a romantic couple making good decisions about their sexual choices—in their actions, thoughts, and words. But I couldn't find one.*

➤ How would you define purity? Impurity?

➤ Can you think of any current, popular movies where the characters make a conscious decision to refrain from sex outside of marriage, to avoid tempting situations, or to behave, dress, or speak in a way that discourages sexual topics rather than encourages them?

➤ Do you think producers of movies—and other media—make a conscious attempt to promote sexual immorality? If so, what do you think the reason might be?

➤ When you watch a movie that has sexual content—even a brief scene—that doesn't fit into God's design (sex before marriage, adultery), do you consider that movie to be outside of God's desires for us? Explain your reasoning.

Get out while you can; get out of this sick and stupid culture!
—*from Acts 2,* The Message

➤ Why is it okay—or not okay—to expose yourself to movies, videos, TV, et cetera, that contain sexual content?

➤ What might God say if you asked him whether it's okay for you to watch, see, read, or listen to something that has sexual content? A lot of sexual content? Explain where your ideas come from if you can.

option [individual activity]
**Keepin' Clean**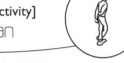

This activity will provide your guys with a chance to make a few, specific goals regarding their sexual integrity and inner purity. The combination of a narrowed playing field and personal choices will make this personal, challenging, and doable for your teens.

Give each student a copy of **Keepin' Clean** (page 76) and a pen. Explain that they should list three actions they desire to do or *not* do to maintain their inner purity. Let them know whether their list will be private or whether your teens will be pairing up and sharing their plans with accountability partners. It's a good idea to have established a high degree of trust among group members if you plan to have them share. Encourage them to move to a private spot in the room or nearby. Discourage small talk during this time, and play music while they're writing.

When they've finished, move on with—

*Your plan is between you and God. He knows what you've committed to, and he promises to provide the strength you need to follow through. But you must want his help and ask for it. If you try to do this alone, you'll fall short somewhere along the line.*

If you're having your guys pair up as accountability partners, let them meet for a few minutes to review the plans. Encourage them to check in with each other regularly.

Pass out the envelopes. Have your guys put their handouts in the envelopes and seal them. Encourage them to bring the list home and reread it regularly, maybe at the beginning of each week.

## Bible study
# Gettin' into the Word

**David and Bathsheba**
2 Samuel 11:1-17

**You'll need—**

• Bibles

 **Nudgers** (nuj´erz) *n.* a tool used to gently push teens toward new insight

- All of David's troubles started with a bad decision—to stay home while the other men went to war.
- David's second mistake was allowing himself to continue admiring Bathsheba beyond that first glance.
- David's third mistake was to move beyond admiring to imagining.
- David's fourth mistake was sending a servant to get Bathsheba.
- David's fifth mistake was ignoring God's law against adultery.
- David's mistakes snowballed from there—illegitimate pregnancy, deceit, cover-up, and murder.
- David assumed Uriah was as interested in sleeping with Bathsheba as David had been.
- David hadn't counted on the fact that Uriah was a man of true integrity.
- After repeatedly failing to break Uriah's integrity, David did the next best thing—he had him killed.
- And there's not a single conversation between David and God in verses 1-17.

Move into the lesson with something like this—

*The reason it's so important to have a plan for protecting yourself sexually—inside and out—is because without a solid commitment to purity, it's far* *too easy to walk into a bad situation and not even want to get out. David, one of the Bible's most disciplined, wise, and godly men, faced that very temptation and caved.*

Have your students read 2 Samuel 11:1-17 to themselves. Then have four students read the parts of David, the messenger, Uriah, and the narrator. When finished, discuss the following questions—

- List David's actions between catching his first glimpse of Bathsheba and sleeping with her.
- Name all the points where David had an opportunity to alter the chain of events. What could he have done differently?
- There's no sign that David was talking with God during these events. How might that be significant to the story?
- Thousands of years after this took place, everyone still remembers David. What about Uriah? What do you think of his role and his choices in this story? What can you learn from him?

Close with some comments along these lines—

*We all know our thoughts can be wicked while at the same time our actions can appear to be Christ-like. Being pure means that both our thoughts and our actions are pure. Purity is not something we hope for. It's something we pursue. It requires conscious effort and wise decisions at every intersection. The first decision seldom leads to a crash; a series of*

Summing it all up, friends, I'd say you'll do best by filling your minds and meditating on things true, noble, reputable, authentic, compelling, gracious—the best, not the worst; the beautiful, not the ugly; things to praise, not things to curse.

—*from Philippians 4*, The Message

**quote**

 "I've learned that what you are thinking about, you are becoming."

—*age 55*

decisions does. The first good choice we make has to be followed by a whole series of others to stay on the right road.

Everywhere you look in today's world, a sexually tempting photo, story, Web site, advertisement, or movie beckens. Protecting your heart's purity means actively guarding your eyes, your ears, and your mind all the time. You have to be willing to do whatever it takes. This is a lifelong process, but an important one. Here are a few tips—

> Some issues may be a struggle all your life. Don't give up.

> Pick one area of your life to work on at first. Don't tackle all your difficulties at once.

> Lasting change usually happens in small steps. Start small, be consistent, and be tenacious.

> Accountability—having a friend who will ask you hard questions about your life—helps you in your pursuit of purity. You have to open your life to another person. You have to find an accountability partner. Go for it!

> Take heart. God knows your struggles. He will help you in your pursuit of purity and godliness.

> Jesus continuously offers forgiveness. Anytime you fail, he'll give you a fresh start.

— closing —
# Takin' It to Heart

Give each student a copy of **The Next Step—Becoming a Man with a Pure Heart** (page 77). Share an example or two of key ideas if you like. Allow some time to fill out the handouts and review their responses. Remind them to keep their papers where they can review them during the week.

This is a lesson when it may be important to give your guys an opportunity for silent confession. You can also ask for several volunteers to pray for the group members or lead with a prayer like this yourself—

Lord, you know about our struggles with purity and you know our failures. One by one, we confess them to you you now. Forgive us for every one of these sins. [pause] Help us look to you for the strength we need against temptations, especially sexual temptations. Help us to live godly lives, the same on the inside as on the outside. We want to bring honor to you. In Jesus' name, amen.

You're blessed when you get your inside world—your mind and heart—put right. Then you can see God in the outside world.
—Jesus from Matthew 5, The Message

But don't think you've preserved your virtue simply by staying out of bed. Your *heart* can be corrupted by lust even quicker than you *body*. Those leering looks you think nobody notices—they also corrupt.
—Jesus from Matthew 5, The Message

All handouts are posted at
www.YouthSpecialties.com/free/guys
in plain text, Rich Text Format,
MS Word 95/6.0, and PDF formats.
Buyers of *Guys* can use them for *free!*

# And the Winner Is...

As a group, come up with your top selections for the following categories. You must all agree on the choices.

*Favorite movies*

1.

2.

3.

4.

5.

*Favorite television shows*

1.

2.

3.

4.

5.

*Favorite female celebrities*

1.

2.

3.

4.

5.

What qualities do you want in a movie that you like to watch over and over again? Make of list.

# IS GOD COOL WITH THIS?

After each item, decide whether God is cool with the activity (a definite yes for Christians), he's tweaked by it (a definite no-no for Christians), or something in between. Place an X on each scale to indicate your rating.

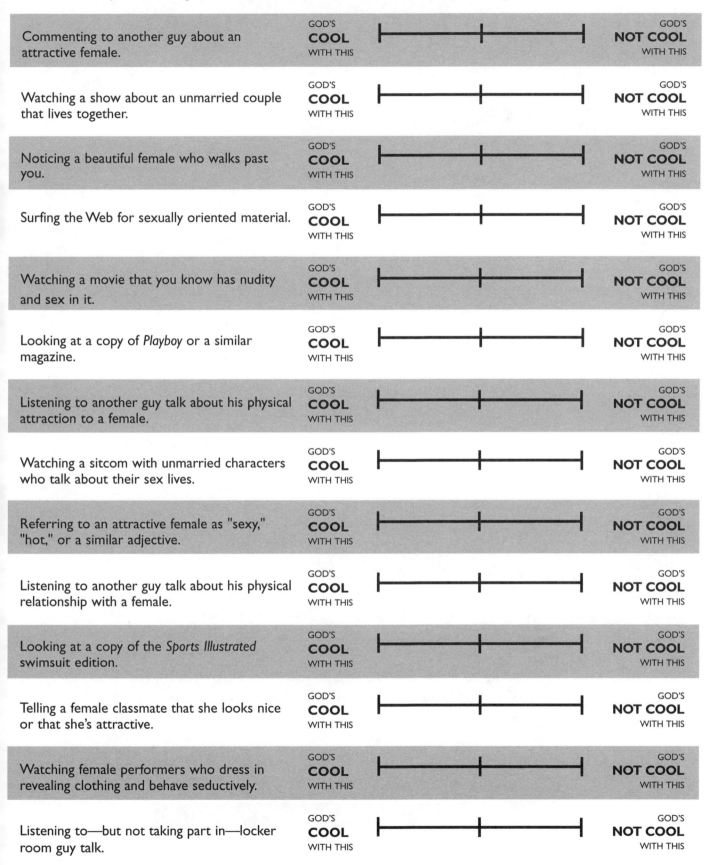

Commenting to another guy about an attractive female.

GOD'S **COOL** WITH THIS — GOD'S **NOT COOL** WITH THIS

Watching a show about an unmarried couple that lives together.

GOD'S **COOL** WITH THIS — GOD'S **NOT COOL** WITH THIS

Noticing a beautiful female who walks past you.

GOD'S **COOL** WITH THIS — GOD'S **NOT COOL** WITH THIS

Surfing the Web for sexually oriented material.

GOD'S **COOL** WITH THIS — GOD'S **NOT COOL** WITH THIS

Watching a movie that you know has nudity and sex in it.

GOD'S **COOL** WITH THIS — GOD'S **NOT COOL** WITH THIS

Looking at a copy of *Playboy* or a similar magazine.

GOD'S **COOL** WITH THIS — GOD'S **NOT COOL** WITH THIS

Listening to another guy talk about his physical attraction to a female.

GOD'S **COOL** WITH THIS — GOD'S **NOT COOL** WITH THIS

Watching a sitcom with unmarried characters who talk about their sex lives.

GOD'S **COOL** WITH THIS — GOD'S **NOT COOL** WITH THIS

Referring to an attractive female as "sexy," "hot," or a similar adjective.

GOD'S **COOL** WITH THIS — GOD'S **NOT COOL** WITH THIS

Listening to another guy talk about his physical relationship with a female.

GOD'S **COOL** WITH THIS — GOD'S **NOT COOL** WITH THIS

Looking at a copy of the *Sports Illustrated* swimsuit edition.

GOD'S **COOL** WITH THIS — GOD'S **NOT COOL** WITH THIS

Telling a female classmate that she looks nice or that she's attractive.

GOD'S **COOL** WITH THIS — GOD'S **NOT COOL** WITH THIS

Watching female performers who dress in revealing clothing and behave seductively.

GOD'S **COOL** WITH THIS — GOD'S **NOT COOL** WITH THIS

Listening to—but not taking part in—locker room guy talk.

GOD'S **COOL** WITH THIS — GOD'S **NOT COOL** WITH THIS

**Blessed Are the Pure in Heart**

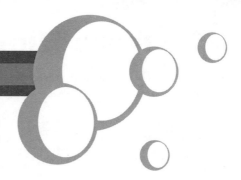

# Keepin' Clean

Think about how you can protect your inner purity. List three specific ideas about what you *will* or what you *will not* do to avoid impure thoughts.

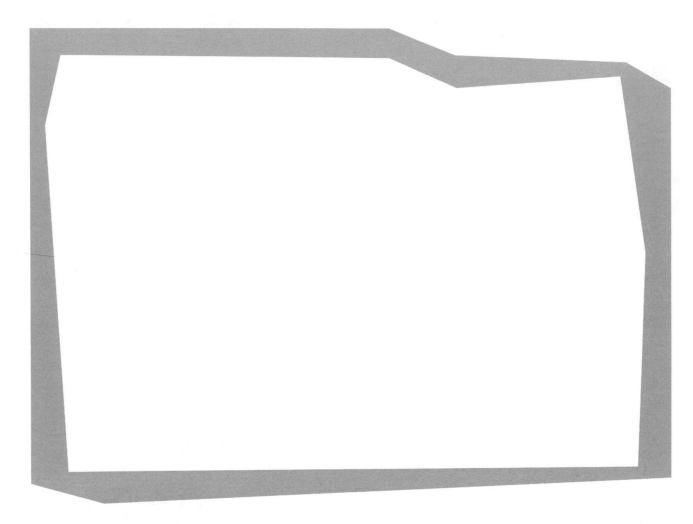

Summing it all up, friends, I'd say you'll do best by filling your minds and meditating on things true, noble, reputable, authentic, compelling, gracious—the best, not the worst; the beautiful, not the ugly; things to praise, not things to curse.

**—from Philippians 4, The Message**

Think about the lesson we've just finished. List four or five key ideas that stand out the most.

1. _____

2. _____

3. _____

4. _____

5. _____

Which idea on your list is the most important to you? Circle it.

## Take Action

What are specific actions or steps you can take to make your circled idea a reality?

1. _____

2. _____

3. _____

## 🔆 THE ISSUE

Male friendships aren't about hugging trees and barking at the moon with a group of fellow birthday-suited guys...at least not totally. It's about finding—and being—that friend who sticks closer than a brother.

---

┌ introduction ┐
## Delvin' In

Guy friendships have an entirely different aura than girl friendships. Think for a moment: how often do guys hug each other just because one or the other needs a little bit of encouragement, call one another on the phone to chat about anything and everything, send each other notes or e-mails just to say hi?

What you see instead are high fives, a slap after a touchdown, good-natured wrestling, grabbing a hat for a quick game of keep-away, a punch in the ribs to make a point, knuckle-to-knuckle bonking as an expression of congratulations. They need and want friendships just like girls, but the expression is different—physical, tough, sparring.

Guys are more likely to build relationships on shared physical experiences—sports, music, computers, and risk taking—and less on shared verbal experiences. Boys use action to develop relational security. They find their place among their peers with others who are comfortable with the same level of physical aggressiveness, risk, and activity.

Guy friendships may be difficult to develop, but the need for them is real. Use this session to help your guys build solid friendships with other guys.

**quote**

"A faithful friend is an image of God."
—*French proverb*

┌ opening activity ┐
## Warmin' Up

**The Friendship Gamble**

When your guys arrive, give them a quick refresher in poker hands—

**You'll need—**
• **One deck of Uno game cards**

actually these are modified poker hands. (No, they're not going to play poker. You're using Uno cards.) These are the sets they need to know—

> pair (two of the same number, any color)
> three of a kind (three of the same number, any color)
> run (three cards in sequential order, any color)
> flush (five cards of the same color, any numbers)
> straight flush (five cards of the same color, in sequential order)
> full house (one pair plus three of a kind)

Hand out between two and five cards to each student, five if your group is small, fewer if your group is large. If your group is on the smaller side, be sure you can make several combinations of each set with the cards you give out. Explain to the guys that when you call a set, such as three of a kind or full house, they must group up with other guys to create it. Even if a student has all the necessary cards by himself, he *must* group up with at least one other person. The first group to form the correct hand wins that round.

Call out the next hand. Play about 10 rounds (more or less as your time allows). When you've finished, collect the cards and talk about the activity—

> How did you figure out who you needed to group up with?
> If there were two different people whose cards would have given you the winning hand, how did you decide between the two?
> In real life, how do you decide who you want to group up with or be friends with?
> If you're friends with several different groups of guys, how do you decide who you'll spend time with?

Laugh with your happy friends when they're happy; share tears when they're down. Get along with each other; don't be stuck-up. Make friends with nobodies; don't be the great somebody.
—*from Romans 12,* The Message

## exploring the topic
# Diggin' a Little Deeper

Move into the next activity with some comments like these—

> *Your friends are probably some of the most important people in your life. Friendships play a role in defining who you are now, and they play a role in defining who you're becoming.*
>
> *We're going to look at friendship more closely to see how God defines it and to see what we can do to be a better friend.*

Choose one or more of the following options—

option [group activity]
Things Guys Do

Divide your guys into groups of four or five. Give each group a copy of **Things Guys Do**

**You'll need—**
- Copies of **Things Guys Do** (page 84), **one for each group**
- Pens

(page 84) and a pen. Explain that they'll have five minutes to come up with as many answers as they can for each of the three categories.

When time is up, ask the groups to read some or all of their lists. Then discuss the following questions—

> What are the differences between the activities in your do-with-a-group and do-with-one-or-two-friends lists?
> What are the differences between the activities in your do lists and your don't-do lists?
> Do your lists reflect male friendships only or those of teens in general? Why do you think so?
> Compare the friendships girls tend to have with the friendships guys tend to have. Explain the similarities and differences.

option [video clip discussion]
Remember the Titans—
Friendship

Show the clip beginning when Gary, celebrating the team's victory, is involved in a car accident. His friend Julius visits him in the hospital.

**1:25:40** Gary is driving past high school fans on Main Street.
**1:29:24** "Left side, strong side."

Follow up with these questions and others you may want to ask—

> What did the guys say or do to express how they felt about each other?
> In what ways did the guys seem uncomfortable with each other or the circumstances they found themselves in?
> How do teen guys usually communicate their thoughts and feelings with their best buddies?
> Why is it difficult for guys to be open and honest with others, even their friends?

A friend is always loyal.
—*Proverbs 17:17,* NLT

option [individual activity]
## Top 10

For either quote, ask—

> What do you think this statement means? Do you agree or disagree with it? Talk about your thoughts.

Then discuss this question—

> Why should accountability—encouraging your friends to make good decisions and to follow through with their decisions—be an important part of our friendships? How can you set up an accountability relationship?

Give everyone a copy of **Top Ten** (page 85) and a pen. Say something like—

**You'll need—**
- Copies of **Top Ten** (page 85), one for each guy
- Pens

*There are lots of qualities that are important to look for in a friend. Some of those are listed on this sheet. Rank each quality from 1 to 10 with 1 being the most important. When you're done, we'll see how what our group rankings look like.*

**quote**

"True friends are people who care for one another more 'in spite of' than 'because of.'"
—*Betty Carlson in* Life Is for Living (*quoted in* The Quotable Christian: Favorite Quotes from Notable Christians *compiled by Helen Hosier, Barbour, 1998*)

Give your teens a few minutes to complete the handout. When you're ready, review the list. For each one, ask how many guys chose it as their number one, number two, or number three pick. This will give everyone a general idea of how others view the importance of each item. You can tally the results of you prefer. Ask—

Saul told his son Jonathan and all the attendants to kill David. But Jonathan was very fond of David and warned him.
—1 Samuel 19:1-2

> Which qualities on the list are most difficult in guy friendships? Are those qualities you look for in a friend?

Choose one of the following quotes to discuss*:

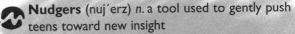

Bible study
## Gettin' into the Word

**Jonathan and David**
Selected passages from 1 Samuel 18-23

**You'll need—**
- Bibles

"In friendship we can bind ourselves too closely. With our demands, hopes, and expectations of the other, we can [inhibit] the potential in our relationships."

"True friendship is not only built on...continually doing things for each other. [This] may in fact exhaust the relationship. Nor is true friendship built on...much-talking and constant self-disclosure. [This] may be more a reflection of insecurity than of trust"

**Nudgers** (nuj′erz) *n.* a tool used to gently push teens toward new insight

> Imagine the parents of your best friend hating you, then liking you, then hating you, then liking you.
> Imagine not being allowed to see or talk to your closest friend.

> Imagine loving a friend so much that you hand over all your inheritance to him.
> Imagine having your best friend being awarded your spot as a starter on a sports team while you are benched.

*Both quotes are from Dare to Journey with Henri Nouwen by Charles Ringma, Piñon Press, 2000, p. 126, 133.

Transition into the Bible study by saying something like this—

*Friendship is an important part of everyone's life. Even when boys are very young, they want to have a companion to play with. Let's look at a famous friendship in the Bible to get some practical ideas for quality friendship.*

Read the following passages and discuss the questions.

**1 Samuel 17:55–18:4** (This event takes place shortly after David killed Goliath.)

> ➤ Why did Jonathan give his robe, tunic, sword, bow, and belt to David?
> ➤ What do you think it means to be "one in spirit" with another person, like Jonathan and David were?
> ➤ How does this happen?
> ➤ Why does this happen?
> ➤ Why is being one in spirit beneficial for a good friendship? Is it essential? Talk about that.

**1 Samuel 18:28–19:7**

> ➤ What did Jonathan risk by going against his father's command and warning David?
> ➤ Describe a time one of your friend went out on a limb for you. What did he risk?
> ➤ Describe a time when you went out on a limb for a friend? Why did you do it?

**1 Samuel 20:1–9**

> ➤ Do most guys have the same amount of loyalty toward their friends as Jonathan and David did? Talk about that.
> ➤ What puts the most stress on guy friendships today?

> ➤ How do you and your friends deal with those stresses? How can you deal with the challenges more effectively?

**1 Samuel 23:15–18**

> ➤ Why is Jonathan's commitment to David so extraordinary? If you were Jonathan, would you be as loyal and committed to David?
> ➤ An old proverb says that one of the most difficult things about friendship is being excited for the other person's successes. What do you think about that?

End the Bible study with comments like this—

*Jonathan and David are perfect examples of what it means to be friends through thick and thin. They spent a lot of time together, but also spent time apart. They talked about problems. They openly expressed their devotion and loyalty. At the news of Jonathan's death, David wrote a song that included the lines, "I grieve for you, Jonathan my brother; you were very dear to me."*

*Their friendship stood the test of both time and trouble. A relationship like that is priceless and worth investing in. To have that kind of friendship, you have to be willing to be that kind of friend.*

So Jonathan made a covenant with the house of David, saying, "May the Lord call David's enemies to account." And Jonathan had David reaffirm his oath out of love for him, because he loved him as he loved himself.
—1 Samuel 20:16-17

**quote**

"To have a good friend is one of the highest delights of life; to be a good friend is one of the noblest and most difficult undertakings."
—*from* God's Little Instruction Book on Friendship *(Honor Books, 1996, page 10)*

# Takin' It to Heart

Since many guys are tribal by nature—desiring to be part of the crowd—create a "blood brother" handshake. A special handshake

**You'll need—**
- **Whiteboard and marker**
- **Copies of The Next Step— Becoming a Man Who Values Friendships** (page 86)
- **Pens**

gives your "tribe" identity, bonds the guys together, and helps each teen feel included.

Start by brainstorming a list of key points from the lesson on a whiteboard. Then think of symbolic gestures that might represent any of the key points, figure out a sequence for the gestures, and review the whole handshake a few times. Keep these points in mind—

- ➤ Create a handshake that has meaning, so your boys are reminded—however subtly—of the truths it represents each time they shake hands.
- ➤ Allow the creative process to be lighthearted to counterbalance the more intense nature of other parts of the session. Put some music on.
- ➤ If your team responds well to this activity, use the handshake with each boy the next time you see him and continue to use the handshake so it becomes the group's greeting.

**quote**

"A friend is someone with whom you can be one hundred percent yourself."
—from God's Little Instruction Book on Friendship (Honor Books, 1996)

Give each teen a copy of **The Next Step— Becoming a Man Who Values Friendships** (page 86). Share an example or two of key ideas if you like. Allow some time to fill out the handouts and review their responses. Remind them to keep their papers where they can review them during the week.

Close the session with prayer, perhaps drawing close together and putting a hand on the shoulder of a neighbor.

*Lord, we all want good friends, real friends, true friends…friends like Jonathan and David. Bring those kinds of friendships into our lives by helping us to be the kind of friend we want to have. Use today's session to change our lives. Amen.*

Jonathan said to David, "Go in peace, for we have sworn friendship with each other in the name of the Lord."
—1 Samuel 20:42

All handouts are posted at
www.YouthSpecialties.com/free/guys
in plain text, Rich Text Format,
MS Word 95/6.0, and PDF formats.
Buyers of *Guys* can use them for *free!*

# Things Guys Do

In five minutes, come up with as many ideas as you can for the categories listed below.

| Things guys do with a group of friends | Things guys do with one or two friends | Things guys *don't* do with a group of friends | Things guys *don't* do with one or two friends |
|---|---|---|---|
| go to a football game<br><br>play pool | watch TV<br><br>play video games | bake cookies<br><br>meet at the coffee shop for lattés | discuss their girl problems<br><br>go shopping |

# Top Ten

Rank the items in the following lists from one (most important) to 10 (least important).
You can only use each number once.

| Top Ten Traits of a Friend | Top Ten Characteristics of a Friendship |
| --- | --- |
| ☐ Loyal | ☐ Lots of time together |
| ☐ Good athlete | ☐ Accountable to each other |
| ☐ Common interests and hobbies | ☐ Honest with each other |
| ☐ Nice parents | ☐ Not easily offended |
| ☐ Christian | ☐ Time spent apart |
| ☐ Sense of humor | ☐ Discussions on deep issues of life |
| ☐ Good communicator | ☐ Personal boundaries and space |
| ☐ Popular | ☐ Common faith |
| ☐ Generous | ☐ Same ethics and values |
| ☐ Intelligent | ☐ Good times and laughter |

List other characteristics you think should be included in the lists.

| Friend | Friendship |
| --- | --- |
| | |

Think about the lesson we've just finished. List four or five key ideas that stand out the most.

1. _____

2. _____

3. _____

4. _____

5. _____

Which idea on your list is the most important to you? Circle it.

## Take Action

What are specific actions or steps you can take to make your circled idea a reality?

1. _____

2. _____

3. _____

# 8

# The Perfect Storm
## How anger can take guys by surprise

## ◔ THE ISSUE

Headlines of the last several years, most notably the many high school shootings, speak volumes about the anger teen guys are dealing with. A combination of increased testosterone levels during adolescence, the influence of media and technology, and emotional disconnectedness all play roles in the increasing anger guys experience.

### introduction
# Delvin' In

Among the many buzzwords that have been coined in the last decade or so, one specifically conveys strong implications about a widespread crisis—anger management.

Why are so many individuals taking courses, seminars, and lectures, and attending retreats that address this issue? Is the issue of personal anger a new one in the history of mankind? Or is this generation simply being more proactive about addressing it? It personal anger a cross-generational and genderless issue? Or is it more prone to rear its ugly head in males or females of a certain age group?

> Get rid of all bitterness, rage and anger, brawling and slander, along with every form of malice.
>
> *—Ephesians 4:31*

Lately, a lot has been discussed, observed, and theorized about what seems to be the increased displays of violent anger and rage in today's youth, especially boys. In response to the March 2001 fatal school shooting at Santana High School in Santee, California, Michael Kimmel, professor of sociology at State University of New York at Stony Brook, noted in a *Minneapolis Star Tribune* editorial—

> We continue to speak about "teen violence," "youth violence" and "school violence" without ever noticing the fact that the vast majority of the "teens" and "youth" we're talking about are boys.

Gender is the single most obvious and intractable difference when it comes to violence in America.

People are quite willing to point the finger at any number of possible causes—violent video games, broken homes, poverty, and a "culture saturated in images of heroic and redemptive violence" (Kimmel). Some of the problems stem from the changes in cultures over the centuries. Michael Gurian writes in *The Wonder of Boys*—

> There is a definite correlation between competition and aggression, and then also between these and anger—a correlation that previous cultures, when they trained soldiers, understood. In Roman culture, for instance, a soldier's anger was part of his sacred energy, and that anger needed to be encouraged in him so he could be more aggressive in battle. By the same token, when Roman cultures initiated boys into manhood, the elders, fathers, and teachers *taught the boys where and when the anger was to be appropriately expressed.* In other words, the boy didn't just learn competition and aggression in male culture; he also learned "anger management" *(page 30)*

Gurian goes on to say that adults must provide boys with and teach boys about appropriate ways to express anger, especially in light of today's culture in which military and similar training is diminishing.

So what's your role? Simply this—to help your guys recognize the potential each one has for anger, to teach them God's guidelines and suggestions for dealing with anger, and to encourage them to work with one another in forming some simple anger-management strategies they can put into use immediately.

## opening activity
# Warmin' Up

**Face-to-Face Anger**

Begin by identifying anger as a universal and common emotion. Everyone in the room

**You'll need—**
• **Whistle**

has been angry at times. What makes one person angry may or may not make another person angry. The actions that result from angry feelings can range from shrugging it off to yelling to breaking something to inflicting physical pain.

Use this activity as a way to help your guys express what makes them feel anger. They will talk to a single person at a time. The pace is quick.

Instruct the guys to partner with one other person. Read the first item in the list below. Both students should give a response, one at a time. Remind them to pay attention to their partners' responses for the follow-up discussion. After a few seconds, blow the whistle as a signal to get a new partner. Only give them a few seconds to pair up again. (You may want to arrange your teens in two concentric circles so that with each switch one circle moves to the next person on the left. This prevents students from feeling left out and is more efficient timewise.) Read the second item and repeat the process. Be sure they understand they have to give first-thought answers as the time will be brief.

> Name something your parents do that makes you angry.
> Name something a teacher does that makes you angry.
> Without naming the friend, name something a friend does that makes you angry.

> Name something at school that makes you angry.
> Name something you do that makes you angry.
> Name a rule at home or school that makes you angry.
> Name something that made you angry today.
> Name something that makes you angry every single time it happens.
> Name something that makes you angry sometimes, but not all the time.
> Name a small, insignificant thing that makes you angry.
> Name something that makes *you* angry but not others.
> Name something that makes other people angry but not you.
> Say a phrase that makes you angry whenever you hear it.

When you've finished the list, ask the guys to share some of the answers they heard without mentioning any names. Then discuss the following questions—

> What similarities did you notice about what makes us angry?
> It can be difficult to think of answers quickly. What answers have you thought of that you didn't get to mention earlier?
> Did any of your own answers surprise you? Talk about that.
> Why is it a good idea to talk about your anger with others?

**quote**

"About 20 percent of all violent crime is committed by children under the age of eighteen; most of those offenders, whether jailed or not, return to committing crimes; 90 percent of these offenders are boys."
—*Michael Gurian in* The Wonder of Boys *(Tarcher/Putnam, 1996, page 183)*

## exploring the topic
# Diggin' a Little Deeper

Transition with some comments like this—

***Anger isn't a new emotion or response. Cain was angry when Abel's***

*sacrifice was more pleasing to God than his. God was angry when the people of Noah's time lived corrupt and unrighteous lives. The Bible is filled with stories of people being angry at other people and of God being angry with people for their wickedness. Not all anger is the same. Some is justified. Some isn't. Some results in sin. Some doesn't. Some is violent. Some isn't. Human anger, though, always has the potential to end in sin.*

The Lord looked with favor on Abel and his offering, but on Cain and his offering he did not look with favor. So Cain was very angry, and his face was downcast. And while they were in the field, Cain attacked his brother Abel and killed him.

—Gen. 4:4-5, 8

Choose one or more of the following options.

option [group activity]
## Five Faces of Anger

Divide your students into groups of three or four. Distribute **Five Faces of Anger** (page 93) and pens to the groups. Review the brief descriptions of each different kind of anger on the handout. Have your teens give an example or two of each kind of anger listed—hypothetical, from the Bible, or from their own experience.

> **You'll need—**
>
> • Copies of **Five Faces of Anger** (page 93), one for each group
> • Pens

Give them about 10 minutes to work on this. Then gather together and ask for a few examples from each of the different categories. After that, discuss the following—

> ➤ In your experience, what kinds of anger are the most common?
> ➤ God never said, "Thou shalt not be angry." When might human anger be acceptable in God's eyes?
> ➤ How does a person who tends to carry pent up anger change into a person who works out his anger in a godly way?
> ➤ Identify the different kinds of anger in your own life.
> ➤ How might knowing the kinds of anger you're prone to help you deal with anger?

option [video clip discussion]
## Remember the Titans—Anger

First show the clip when the football players react to the news of a riot in which a black teen is shot.

**0:00:00** Opening scene
**0:04:29** "To learn from the best."

After this clip ask a few questions—

> ➤ Why do the football players immediately run to the scene of the action?
> ➤ What do you suppose they intended to do?
> ➤ Describe their coach's reaction to the events.
> ➤ How might Coach Boon have been able to control his anger in the face of all those negative and derogatory comments from the other coach?

**0:18:35** Julias is hanging the poster in his room
**0:20:33** "Let's go to work."

Let the coach's words sink in and speak for themselves as you turn off the VCR and turn to the next activity.

**quote**

"We continue to speak about 'teen violence,' 'youth violence,' and 'school violence' without ever noticing the fact that the vast majority of the 'teens' and 'youth' we're talking about are boys."
—*Michael Kimmel editorial in the* Minneapolis StarTribune *(March 18, 2001)*

option [individual activity]
The Price of an Eye

## Bible study
# Gettin' into the Word

**Cain and Abel**
Genesis 4:1-12

Give each teen a copy of **The Price of an Eye** (page 94) and a pen. Say something like this—

**You'll need—**

- Copies of **The Price of an Eye** (page 94), one for each student
- Pens

> *In the New Testament, Jesus said, "Here's another old saying that deserves a second look: 'Eye for eye, tooth for tooth.' Is that going to get us anywhere? Here's what I propose: 'Don't hit back at all'"* [Matthew 5:38, *The Message*].
>
> *Jesus isn't saying that it's wrong to defend yourself if you're in danger or being harmed. He's saying that taking revenge on someone because you're angry at them for what they did is not the way to live. It's the action—like hitting—or lack of action—like the silent treatment—that follows anger that's usually wrong.*

Give your students several minutes to think about the information and questions on **The Price of an Eye**. When they've finished, discuss the following questions—

- ➤ How does our culture tell or show teen guys to deal with their anger? Talk about that.
- ➤ Do our culture's ways tend to ease the problem or make more trouble or something in between? Talk about your ideas.
- ➤ How do you usually deal with your anger?
- ➤ What are some ways that you and a friend can help each other deal with anger?
- ➤ What situations or people can you—or should you—avoid to help control your anger?

After finishing the Diggin' a Little Deeper activities, say something like this—

**You'll need—**

- 3 copies of **Am I My Brother's Keeper?** (page 95)

> *Anger, especially for males, has the potential to be out of control. In general, men are instinctively competitive and protective, among other things. Those can be positive traits. Being competitive can push a guy to do his best in everything. Being protective can push a guy to watch out for those who are weaker or in need.*
>
> *But those characteristics can also be negative. Being too competitive can cause a guy to do whatever it takes to get ahead of everyone else, no matter how hurtful or unethical. Being too competitive can also make him angry at someone who is better than him in certain areas. Being too protective can cause a guy to overreact to actions that happen to his friends. Being too protective can make a guy angry when someone hurts or ridicules the person he loves the most, namely himself.*
>
> *Let's look at a story in the Bible that deals with those very problems.*

Ask for three volunteers to read **Am I My Brother's Keeper?** (page 95), the scripted story of Cain and Abel. When they've finished, ask for a volunteer to tell what happens next (the end of the story) or read Genesis 3:8-12 as an epilogue. Follow up with questions like these—

- ➤ How did Cain view his relationship with his brother?
- ➤ How did Abel view his relationship with his brother?

- ➤ Why was Cain so angry with his brother that he killed him?
- ➤ How could Cain have dealt with his anger differently?
- ➤ Describe the difference between the anger Cain felt toward Abel and the anger God felt toward Cain.
- ➤ Compare the short-term gain of Cain's actions (Abel is out of the way) to the long-term cost of Cain's actions (permanent banishment and wandering).
- ➤ What changes do you want to make in the way you deal with anger? Who can you ask to help you?

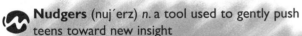

**Nudgers** (nuj´erz) *n.* a tool used to gently push teens toward new insight

- ➤ Cain viewed worship through offerings as a competitive sport.
- ➤ Cain offered a sacrifice without faith. Abel offered a sacrifice by faith.
- ➤ Cain directed his guilt and anger at Abel rather than at himself.
- ➤ Cain allowed his anger to keep simmering rather than let it cool down.
- ➤ Cain's anger resulted in an action that affected the rest of his life.

- ➤ Imagine how much jealousy it would take to move a person to murder.
- ➤ Imagine Jesus showing compassion toward the hemorrhaging woman who drew power from him without permission.
- ➤ Imagine Jesus honoring the prostitute who "defiled" him by wiping his feet with her hair.
- ➤ Imagine Jesus forgiving those who persecuted him.

Close with something like this—

> *Anger is extremely powerful. If we let it control our thoughts and actions, it has the potential to ruin our lives. This is an area that must be controlled. Not only does it take effort and determination on our parts, but also a willingness to submit to the Lord and let him work in this area.*

But now you must rid yourselves of all such things as these: anger, rage, malice, slander, and filthy language from your lips.
—*Colossians 3:8*

— closing —
# Takin' It to Heart

Give each teen a copy of **The Next Step— Becoming a Man of Self-Control** (page 96). Share an example

**You'll need—**
- **Copies of The Next Step— Becoming a Man of Self-Control** (page 96)

or two of key ideas if you like. Allow some time to fill out the handouts and review their responses. Remind them to keep their papers where they can review them during the week.

Before praying together, read the following excerpt from *Answering God* by Eugene Peterson (HarperSanFrancisco, 1989). This will encourage you and your guys to include prayer as the number one ingredient in anger management.

> It is easy to be honest before God with our hallelujahs; it is somewhat more difficult to be honest in our hurts; it is nearly impossible to be honest before God in the dark emotions of our hate [and anger]. So we commonly suppress our negative emotions…We must pray

In your anger do not sin; when you are on your beds, search your hearts and be silent.

—*Psalm 4:4*

> who we actually are, not who we think we should be. In prayer, all is not sweetness and light. The way of prayer is not to cover our unlovely emotions so that they will appear respectable, but expose them so that they can be enlisted in the work of the kingdom. "It is an act of profound faith to entrust one's most precious hatreds [and anger] to God, knowing they will be taken seriously."

Ask a few guys to pray for the group. Here are some ideas for them—

> - Pray for a better understanding of anger.
> - Pray for the courage to confront angry emotions for what they are and not justify them.

> - Pray for God's help with controlling angry thoughts without simply suppressing them.
> - Pray for wisdom in looking for godly ways to express anger.

Refrain from anger and turn from wrath; do not fret—it leads only to evil.

—*Psalm 3*

All handouts are posted at
www.YouthSpecialties.com/free/guys
in plain text, Rich Text Format,
MS Word 95/6.0, and PDF formats.
Buyers of *Guys* can use them for *free!*

# Five Faces of Anger

Think of one or two examples for each type of anger. The examples can be from the Bible or personal experience, or they can be made up.

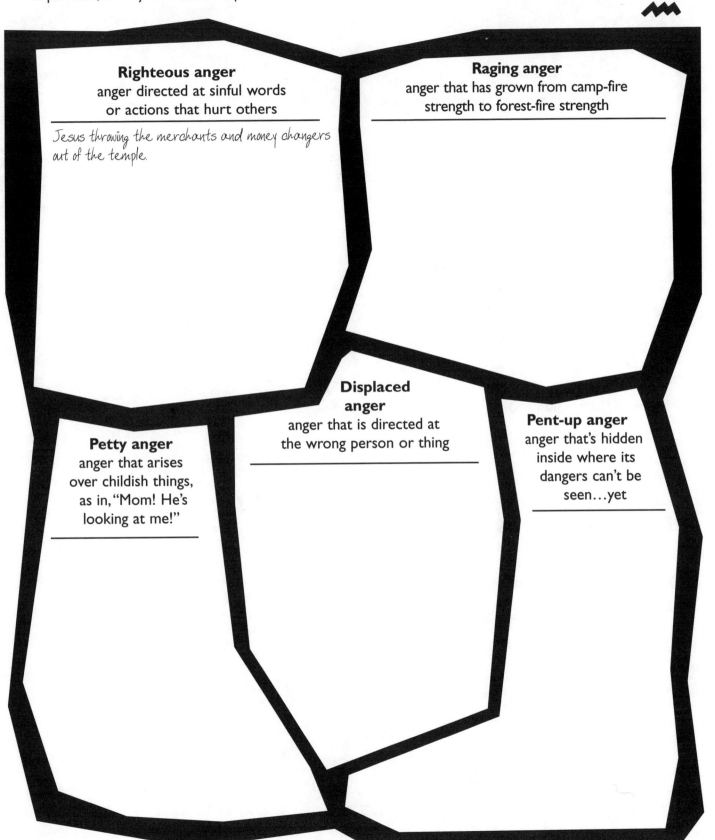

**Righteous anger**
anger directed at sinful words
or actions that hurt others

*Jesus throwing the merchants and money changers out of the temple.*

**Raging anger**
anger that has grown from camp-fire
strength to forest-fire strength

**Petty anger**
anger that arises
over childish things,
as in, "Mom! He's
looking at me!"

**Displaced
anger**
anger that is directed at
the wrong person or thing

**Pent-up anger**
anger that's hidden
inside where its
dangers can't be
seen…yet

# The Price of an Eye

Check all of the appropriate boxes.

## My usual response to anger is to—

- ☐ bottle it up inside
- ☐ talk about it with a friend
- ☐ confront the person or situation that caused my anger
- ☐ pray
- ☐ ignore it and hope it goes away
- ☐ take revenge
- ☐ slam a door or break something
- ☐ work out the feelings through strenuous activity (washing a car, weight lifting)
- ☐ write about it
- ☐ take my mind off of the situation by doing something else
- ☐ count to 10—then the feeling is gone
- ☐ count to 10 before exploding
- ☐ ❋ other

## Things I'd be willing to try (if I haven't already)—

- ☐ pray
- ☐ ask an adult for advice
- ☐ write in a journal or on my computer
- ☐ take a break from the person or situation
- ☐ wait before responding
- ☐ ask a friend to help me make a good decision
- ☐ ❋ other

> Refrain from anger and turn from wrath.
> Psalm 37:8

> In your anger do not sin; when you are on your beds, search your hearts and be silent.
> Psalm 4:4

> A fool gives full vent to his anger, but a wise man keeps himself under control.
> Proverbs 29:11

> Do not make friends with a hot-tempered man, do not associate with one easily angered.
> Proverbs 22:24

> [Love] is not easily angered, it keeps no record of wrongs.
> 1 Corinthians 13:5

# Am I My Brother's Keeper?

**The Cast**
Cain, the elder brother, a farmer
Abel, the younger brother, a shepherd
God, the creator, a major player in all events

**ABEL:** Hey big brother, are you going to the sacrifice site tomorrow?

**CAIN:** Of course I'm going. Don't forget, I'm older than you and know a lot more about sacrifices and stuff.

**ABEL:** Great. I guess I'll see you there.

**CAIN:** Yeah, you and one of those snotty, nostril-licking lambs. How can you stand the stench?

**ABEL:** Whaddya mean? It's great being a shepherd—all that time out in the fields, enjoying God's creation.

**CAIN:** Spare me. I'm older than you, remember, and I know a lot more…

**ABEL:** *(interrupts him)*…I know. You know a lot more than I do about God and other stuff.

**CAIN:** Right. And don't think I'm going to let you beat me this year.

**ABEL:** What do you mean, "beat you"?

**CAIN:** Don't act so innocent. I know your type—always trying to get on God's good side. Shepherds like you use every dirty trick in the book—shampooing the lamb, grooming the lamb, polishing the lamb's hooves, brushing the lamb's teeth, blowing the lamb's nose. Goody goodies like you make me sick.

*Two days later, at the site for offering sacrifices.*

**ABEL:** *(to God)* I know this lamb is small, but he's the firstborn, the most precious to me. Accept him as a symbol of my respect and honor and love for you.

**CAIN:** *(to God)* Ignore all the lamb nonsense. I've brought you the most beautiful apples you've ever seen. Okay, so they're not very tasty—sour and mushy and ulcer-producing—but hey, they're beautiful enough to be in one of Martha Stewart's centerpieces. In fact, she's already called about them but I said, "Hey, sorry, they're already promised to the big guy upstairs. Catch me next year, little lady." That was pretty religious of me, don't you think? And I called her "little lady" instead of "foxy babe" like last time. You should appreciate that.

**GOD:** I don't care about the outer appearance of a sacrifice. I care about the heart attitude of the person offering the sacrifice.

**CAIN:** Oh man, am I in trouble. That Abel is *so* annoying. Always smiling. Always saying nice things to Mom just to butter her up. Always acting like he respects Dad, as if that were even remotely possible. He thinks he's so great, so perfect, so much better than everyone else. Well, I'll show him a thing or two…

**The Perfect Storm** |

Think about the lesson we've just finished. List four or five key ideas that stand out the most.

1. _____

2. _____

3. _____

4. _____

5. _____

Which idea on your list is the most important to you? Circle it.

### Take Action

What are specific actions or steps you can take to make your circled idea a reality?

1. _____

2. _____

3. _____

# 9

# Wanted: Heroes
## (Super powers not required)

## THE ISSUE

Every young boy has a hero who he wants to talk and dress like, who he imitates, and who he secretly wants to be someday. But somewhere along the way, the heroes disappear, replaced by superstars and celebrities. It's time to bring back the heroes—men who deserve to be looked up to and imitated.

introduction
# Delvin' In

Once upon a time, there was a very old man who died. After a long and healthy life, his 90 years finally caught up with him, and he went to sleep one night for the very last time.

When the town heard what had happened, they began gathering in small groups, here and there, all over town, swapping stories, telling tales, wiping tears of both laughter and sorrow from their eyes. The old man, you see, was well loved. He'd been a school janitor. He'd served in his church. He'd helped his neighbors during harvest. He'd mowed lawns for the widows in town. He'd shoveled the walk in front of the library and post office. He'd sat on the school board for longer than anyone could remember. He'd bounced every new baby in town on his knee. He'd handed out chewing gum to every tyke who was tall enough to tap his knee. He'd stayed married to the same woman for 63 years, raised five children, who'd had 14 grandchildren, who'd had 11 great-grandchildren…so far.

He never traveled the world. Never invented anything. Never won any awards aside from a few blue ribbons at the county fair. Never had his name in the newspaper. Never wrote a book, recorded an album, or gotten paid for doing anything that he considered to be a hobby.

When he died, all 514 people in his town mourned, but that was about it. The rest of the world didn't really notice. But that old man had accomplished what few people do anymore—he'd been a hero to hundreds of young boys whose lives he'd been a part of.

Little boys go through an interesting progression of heroes. It starts with Daddy, Grandpa, and other human beings in their lives, but it quickly moves into the superhero phase. These larger-than-life, fictional creatures become all consuming. There are superhero trading cards, T-shirts, action figures, underwear, stickers, lunch boxes, feature films, and backpacks.

But at some point, the little boys realize their superheroes aren't real. Out go the action figures. Out go the lunch boxes. Out go the underwear. It would be nice if Daddy were around to be a hero again, but he's busy working. Grandpa lives in another state. Uncle Jim works nights and weekends. And Mr. Williams, the neighbor, spends most of his time cussing about whatever chore he happens to be doing at the moment.

Enter the new heroes—superstars, celebrities, professional athletes. What a relief. Our little boys aren't hero-less, after all. There are all of these wonderfully rich and famous men for them to emulate—men who, like the childhood superheroes, seem to have it all. Indeed.

In his book *Heroes,* Harold J. Sala writes, "A national magazine recently featured a story decrying the fact that there are no real heroes for today. The article mentioned a survey of young people who were asked who their heroes were. Their answers primarily included rock stars, sports heroes, and movie personalities." Sala goes on to say that his own personal heroes were all flawed human beings who had three things in common—integrity, commitment to their ideals, and a willingness to stand apart from the crowd.

The Bible has heroes, too. It starts with the "heroes of old" who were, in fact, larger than life—giants whose mothers were human and fathers may have been otherworldly. Then came the flawed—but still larger-than-life—epic heroes of the Old Testament: Noah, Abraham, Joseph, Moses, David, Elijah. Finally, there are the New Testament heroes—Joseph, a carpenter, who is mentioned in only a few verses but who shaped Jesus into a man. Peter, a faithful Jew who never made a big name for himself but introduced the nation of God's people to the Messiah. The other disciples, simple men who spread the gospel. Paul, who endured and persevered for the sake of Christ.

Integrity. Character. Steadfastness. Humility. Honor.

Your guys will mostly learn character through the heroes who model it for them. Help them choose the heroes who are worth learning from.

> Similarly, encourage the young men to be self-controlled. In everything set them an example by doing what is good. In your teaching show integrity, seriousness and soundness of speech that cannot be condemned, so that those who oppose you may be ashamed because they have nothing bad to say about us.
> —Titus 2:6-8

opening activity

# Warmin' Up

## Hero Challenge

Use current heroes to infuse the classic Rock-Paper-Scissors with new enthusiasm

Choose three cultural heroes who will resonate with your guys, say a football player, a wrestler, and a marine. Give each an action, perhaps—

> ➤ **Marine** giving a salute
> ➤ **Wrestler** posing as a muscleman
> ➤ **Football player** throwing a pass

The marine beats the wrestler who beats the football player who beats the marine. (You also can choose select specific sports heroes or celebrities. Just assign each personality an action and decide who beats whom.)

Demonstrate each action or pose. Have your guys pair off. On the count of three, each teen performs the action of one of the heroes. In each pair, the person who wins two out of three continues on in the competition. After each round, winners find new partners and losers move to the edge of the room and root for the remaining players. Continue until you have a winner.

You can choose new characters and actions and play again if you have time.

exploring the topic

# Diggin' a Little Deeper

Transition into the next activity with a few words like—

> *Today we're going to talk about heroes and how to choose them. We all had them when we were kids, and we probably all have one or two now. The challenge is to choose heroes who are worthy of our admiration.*

Choose one or more of the following options.

option [group activity]
Hero Census

Divide your students into groups of four or five. Give each group a copy of **Hero Census** (page 103) and a pen. Have them

**You'll need—**
• Copies of **Hero Census** (page 103), one for each group
• Pens

work together to fill out the chart. After they've finished, let them share their answers with the others. If you want, you can keep a census tally of the following things—

> ➤ Hero mentioned by the most groups
> ➤ Number of superheroes
> ➤ Number of accessories such as capes, guns, masks

Then discuss the following questions with them—

- ➤ Why do a boy's heroes change as he gets older?
- ➤ What do little boys look for in a hero?
- ➤ As a teen, what characteristics are you looking for in a hero? Why those characteristics?
- ➤ What's the difference between a hero and an idol?
- ➤ Why is it important for you to have heroes?

option [video clip discussion]
## Tuesdays with Morrie

Morrie, a retired college professor, is dying of Lou Gehrig's disease. Mitch is a former student of Morrie's whose life has gotten out of control. Mitch visits Morrie on Tuesdays and gradually learns about what really matters. Show the clip.

**0:24:36** Mitch arrives at Morrie's and hears "Java Jive."
**0:30:09** Morrie and Mitch are eating ice cream.

Talk about the scene with questions like these or others of your own—

- ➤ What makes Morrie a hero? Talk about that.
- ➤ Are people like Morrie regarded as heroes today? Why or why not?
- ➤ What can a person like Morrie teach a person like Mitch?
- ➤ Do you have a Morrie in your life? If not, how can you get one?

option [individual activity]
## He's My Hero

Say something like—

**You'll need—**
- **Copies of He's My Hero** (page 104), one for each guy
- Pens

*For Christian guys, our ultimate hero is Jesus. His actions and words are a model of what our lives should be like. But we also need heroes we can watch, talk to, ask questions of, and spend time with. That's the way to learn things. Let's say Billy Graham is one of your heroes. He's certainly worthy of that. But there will be a limit to what you can learn from him because you've never had the chance to observe him daily—how he treats his wife, coworkers, and neighbors; how he conducts his personal affairs; how he spends his money; and so on.*

⊚ **TIP**

**Helping your students identify good role models in their lives is an important part of this lesson. Make every effort to include this option in your session.**

Help your students through the process of picking a hero. Hand out **He's My Hero** (page 104) and a pen to each student. First let them brainstorm a list of all the men in their lives. This step is especially important for your students whose families don't provide godly role models for them. Criteria for the heroes include—

- ➤ Someone old enough to have many life experiences.
- ➤ Someone you can observe and spend time with (not necessarily daily).
- ➤ Someone who attempts to live a godly lifestyle (even though none are perfect).

- A male (not that female heroes are any less worthy. But since this lesson is about looking to a person whose life he'd like to emulate, it's important for your guys to have male heroes who can teach them how to live as a godly man).

### ⊙ TIP
For some kids this activity will take a good dose of direction from the leader. You may need to acknowledge the challenge, frustration, and pain of being heroless. Help them find someone. Pray with them that God will bring heros into their lives. Be a hero for them yourself.

Give your guys plenty of time for this activity. When they've finished, discuss the following questions.

- Explain why you chose the man you did.
- Describe what you've already learned from this man.
- What are you hoping to learn from this man in the future?
- Does a Christian guy have to have a Christian hero? Explain your thoughts.
- Heroes don't only save lives and stop disasters. What day-to-day actions might be considered heroic? Why do you think so?

# Gettin' into the Word

**Noah**
Genesis 6:1-8:22, selected verses

**You'll need—**
• Bibles

**Nudgers** (nuj´erz) *n.* a tool used to gently push teens toward new insight

- At that time, men viewed Nephilim—men of great size and strength—as "the heroes of old." Their name means "fallen ones."
- Nephilim get one verse. Noah gets four chapters.
- Noah "walked with God."
- Imagine building a large boat, in the middle of the desert, in a world that had never seen rain, just because God said so.
- Imagine your neighbors and friends making disparaging comments and ridiculing you.
- Imagine all the work and thought it took to build the ark, to gather all the food and supplies, to care for the animals.
- Imagine spending a year with your wife, your three sons, their three wives, and thousands of animals in a space about the size of a football field.
- A true hero can be locked inside a boat for months on end, and he still trusts God.

The Nephilim were on the earth in those days—and also afterward—when the sons of God went to the daughters of men and had children by them. They were the heroes of old, men of renown.

—*Genesis 6:4*

**quote**

"I've learned that you can't be a hero without taking chances."

—*age 43*

After finishing the previous activity, move into the Bible lesson with a few comments like—

*Some people like heroes who are larger-than-life. They make for good stories and exciting adventures. But the heroes whom you'll learn the most from are the everyday men in your lives. Why? Because they've figured out how to live good, decent, godly lives day in and day out. That's heroic.*

*We're going to look at a plain old guy in the Bible who was hero material.*

Divide the Bible reading into sections. Assign each section to a student to read aloud. Discuss the questions after reading each section or wait and discuss the entire passage after the last reading.

### Genesis 6:1-8

- ➤ People considered Nephilim to be "heroes" and "men of renown." Numbers 13:28 and 33 indicate they were large and strong. That's about all we know about them. Why might the Nephilim have been viewed as men of renown?
- ➤ God is grieved over the wickedness of mankind. What might this say about their "heroism"?

### Genesis 6:9-13

- ➤ How is Noah described? What tasks do you imagine him doing?
- ➤ How is the rest of humanity described? What must life have been like for them?
- ➤ Since God destroyed everyone but Noah, talk about what that means for how *we* live and the choices *we* make.

### Genesis 6:22

- ➤ Talk about the significance of the words *everything* and *just as God commanded*. This verse probably doesn't mean God directed Noah about which sandals to wear and which fruit to eat. What does it mean?

- ➤ Do you know anyone who can be described like Noah is described in this verse? Tell about him or her.

### Genesis 7:1-4

- ➤ Noah's reward for being righteous was to spend more than a year cooped up with—and caring for—all those animals and family members. What would your reaction be in that situation? How was Noah able to endure?

### Genesis 7:5, 13-16

- ➤ Describe what life might have been like on the ark.
- ➤ How might Noah have managed to keep peace under the circumstances?

### Genesis 8:15-22

- ➤ If you'd been in Noah's situation, what would you have done as soon as your feet hit dry land?
- ➤ Notice what Noah did. What does this tell you about him?
- ➤ Noah was a man of character and integrity. What does that mean? What does a person of character and integrity act like today?

**quote**

"I've learned that heroes are the people who do what has to be done when it needs to be done, regardless of the consequences."

—age 77

You may want to summarize by making some comments like these—

*In Hebrews 11, Noah is identified as one of the heroes of our faith. He was a man we could look up to. We can look to him as a role model, even though he wasn't perfect.*

*As we grow older, superheroes fall away because they aren't real. We can't relate to their extraordinary lives, and we know we can't ever* become what they are. We look for other men—real men, godly men—to be our heroes.

When men with integrity, honor, and other godly characteristics come into your life, watch them. Spend time with them. Talk to them. Learn from them.

**TIP**
Show the music video "Secret Ambition" (Michael W. Smith, *Change Your World*, Provident, 1992), the story of the ultimate hero who didn't appear to be a hero at all.

___ End with a time of prayer.

— closing —
# Takin' It to Heart

Give each teen a copy of **The Next Step— Becoming a Man Who Chooses Heroes Wisely** (page 105). Share an example or two of key ideas if you like. Allow some time to fill out the handouts and review their responses. Remind them to keep their papers where they can review them during the week.

**You'll need—**
- Copies of **The Next Step—Becoming a Man Who Chooses Heroes Wisely** (page 105), one for each guy
- Pens

*Lord, thanks for the men of the Bible who are heroes to us. We'll keep looking to them for guidance, but we all need heroes, flesh and blood heroes, whom we can look up to. Men who can teach us how to act, how to love, how to make wise decisions, how to walk in your ways. We need heroes who'll walk with us and challenge us to be godly. Establish a hero in each of our lives whom we can learn from. Thanks for looking out for us! Amen.*

Young men, in the same way be submissive to those who are older. All of you, clothe yourselves with humility toward one another, because "God opposes the proud but gives grace to the humble."
—1 Peter 5:5

# Hero Census

Fill in the following hero information. Try to come up with at least two for each age level.

| | Heroes' Names | Special abilities or powers | Hero accessories or description |
|---|---|---|---|
| **Preschool** | Fireman | Puts out fires | Fire truck, hose |
| **Elementary School** | Batman | Drives the Batmobile | Mask, cape, Batmobile |
| **Junior High** | Tiger Woods | Great athelete, humble, generous | Golf clubs, ball, hat |
| **Now** | | | |

# HE'S MY HERO

Spend time listing all the men who are a part of your life (relatives, teachers, coaches, youth group staff, church attenders, neighbors, friends' parents, bosses, coworkers...)

Go back to your list and circle the names of men who are your top candidates for hero. Pick one whom you would especially like to choose as your hero. He should be—

**Someone** old enough to have many life experiences.

**Someone** you can observe and spend time with (not necessarily daily).

**Someone** who attempts to live a godly lifestyle (even though none are perfect).

## — Fill in the following information about that person —

What's his name?

How do you know him (through school, work, family, etc.)?

How long have you known him?

How often do you spend time with him? How long?

Why do you look to him as a hero (what are his good qualities)?

List five words that describe him.

Describe a specific thing he has said or done that has influenced you positively.

Think about the lesson we've just finished. List four or five key ideas that stand out the most.

1.

2.

3.

4.

5.

Which idea on your list is the most important to you? Circle it.

## Take Action

What are specific actions or steps you can take to make your circled idea a reality?

1.

2.

3.

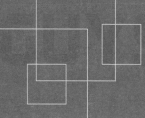

## ◐ THE ISSUE

Young men need a place, a time, and a reason for breaking down the wall between adolescence and young adulthood.

---

### introduction
# Delvin' In

Young people today have very few opportunities to mark the passage from adolescence into adulthood. Graduating from high school and obtaining a driver's license are the two most common rites for American teens. In addition to those, *some* teens experience a first job, a first kiss, confirmation or bar mitzvah, the prom. And then there's that first time using drugs or alcohol and that first sexual encounter.

In *The Wonder of Boys*, Michael Gurian notes that boys desperately want to be part of a tribe, in other words, part of something bigger than themselves that they belong to. A major role of the tribe is to help initiate boys into manhood, one step at a time. The tribe is made up of both peers and elders, and according to Gurian, boys "don't care if that tribe of elders comes from blood relatives, from nonblood elder friends, or from institutions, or, most likely, from some combination of them all. *Boys are simply hungry to become the best men they can be* [italics added] (page 151).

Your guys may have numerous elders in their lives. Or not. They may have a sense of consciously and determinedly taking small steps toward adulthood. Or not. They may already have had a number of significant experiences throughout their time in the church. Or not. Either way, they can never have too many of those things. They can never hear, "You are loved; you are God-created; you are blessed with a purpose; you are one step closer to adulthood," too many times.

In this chapter you'll find plenty of ideas to choose from as you plan this final session. It's up to you to choose what you think will work for the personalities and interests of your guys, for your facility, for your group size, and for your financial resources.

All of the students who offered ideas and suggestions for this chapter repeated common themes—

- ➤ "We love to party" (as in, we love to celebrate).
- ➤ "We love to party, especially if the party's for us.
- ➤ "We love to party, especially it if means free food."
- ➤ "We don't want parties to be cheesy or stupid or boring or serious."
- ➤ When asked what kind of memento, if any, would be meaningful to them, the most common response was, "*Don't get any of those sappy, shallow things that say, like, 'God loves you, now go out and have a blessed day.'* And don't get us all the same thing, unless it's really cool and meaningful."
- ➤ What did they want most of all? In the words of Danny, a sophomore, "I'd want my leader to say something to me personally, something that's just for me. That would mean a ton because then I'd know he was interested in me and that he'd listened to the things I'd said."

So there you have it.

They want a party. They want food. They want a memento—if it's well thought out and meaningful. And they want some individual words of wisdom and encouragement from you.

Make your celebration as simple or as elaborate as you want. Your closing event will probably include—

1. A time for play
2. A time for food
3. A time for reflection and goal setting
4. A time for peer affirmation
5. A time for leader affirmation
6. A time for blessing

## A Time for Play

The purpose of a time for play is to say, "Let's have fun being together just because," "I enjoy hanging out with you," and "God enjoys seeing us laugh and play together."

As noted in the Session 7 introduction, guys tend to bond through physical activity, so what you choose as the framework for this session may have a direct impact on the overall effectiveness of your young men's ability to give and receive affirmations, to reflect, to set goals, and to accept the blessings.

> **You'll need—**
> • Supplies for the activity you choose

> **quote**
> "As a culture, we could use more wholesome rituals for coming of age…We need more positive ways to acknowledge growth, more ceremonies and graduations. It's good to have toasts, celebrations and markers for teens that tell them: You are growing up and we're proud of you."
> —Mary Pipher in Reviving Ophelia (Ballantine, 1994, page 291)

If your guys all have a special interest, consider crafting your session around it.

You may want to package this event into an extended trip—a week, a weekend, overnight, dawn-to-dusk—to go biking, camping, mountain climbing, skiing, surfing, or caving. Or consider a building, music, or computer project. Even a change of scenery helps if you can't get the time or the resources together for something more extensive.

Whether you do this session in your usual setting or as a special event what matters most are the words you speak to your guys, the

> **quote**
> "Rafting trips, ropes courses, and other rites-of-passage experiences need to become regular parts of a boy's adolescence. Through them, boys learn their gold, their spirituality, their shadow, and grow up."
> —Michael Gurian in The Wonder of Boys (Tarcher/Putnam, 1996, page 144)

encouragement you give them, and the honor and acknowledgement you express to them as on-your-way-to-adulthood individuals. Your words of blessing and affirmation are the best gift you can give them.

Here are some guidelines—

> ➤ Monitor competition—or compete as a group against "the last group's" skill, time, whatever. (The last group can be entirely ficticious!)
> ➤ Nothing new, embarrassing, or difficult to master.
> ➤ Leaders participate, not just observe.

Here are other ideas about what to do—

> ➤ Game tournaments—spoons, Uno, Twister, computer races
> ➤ A short video—bloopers, Wallace and Gromit, home movies, cartoons
> ➤ Stupid human tricks
> ➤ Retro fun—Hot Wheels and race tracks, squirt gun tomfoolery, Legos, yo-yos (let your guys reminisce about their "childhoods" through these activities)

## A Time for Food

The purpose of eating together is to gather as a family around the table. You'll have to adapt if you're planning an extended event. Here are some guidelines you may want to use—

> **You'll need—**
> • Food and drinks
> • Plates, silverware, and glasses
> • Tables and chairs
> • CDs and CD player
> • Decorations (optional)

> ➤ Sit, do not mingle.
> ➤ Sit in one group, not in clusters.

- Encourage table talk. (Supply a basketful of conversation-starter questions on strips of paper to pass around if you think your guys will need help.)
- Have a go-for-the-gusto dessert!
- Put on background music.

Here are ideas about how to organize the meal—

- BYOF—bring your own food.
- Have students and leaders pack up or pick up a meal before the meeting.
- Get take-out food.
- Parent-run potluck
- Leader-run potluck
- Leader-supplied home-cooked meal (strongly discouraged by an overwhelming majority of youth workers)

## A Time for Reflection and Goal Setting

The purpose of reflection and goal setting is to look back at the issues and discussions of the previous nine weeks, to think about ways to implement positive changes in attitudes and actions, and to set reasonable goals for putting faith into practice. Here are some guidelines—

> **You'll need—**
> - Copies of **Breaking Down the Wall** (page 113), one for each guy (optional)
> - Pens
> - Writing paper and envelopes, one for each guy (optional)
> - CD and CD player

- Don't sneak in additional topics—the guys have plenty to think about already.
- No preachy reviews.
- Develop positive goals (I'll say nice things about others), not negative ones (I'll stop harassing dweebs).

Here are ideas about what to do. Put music on while your teens are writing.

### Individual reflection

Give each teen a copy of **Breaking Down the Wall** (page 113) and a pen. Give them some time to think about and write their responses. You can let the guys keep the sheets or you can collect them and use them as a tool for writing encouraging notes, asking relevant questions, and staying connected with each other.

### Individual challenge

Have each teen write a letter to himself about areas he wants to be reminded of or encouraged about in six or eights weeks. Funky writing paper will make this more fun. They should address themselves as a third party.

> Dear Jay,
>
> How are you? How are things going with your brother? I know that sometimes it gets pretty rough sharing a room without feeling like you want to kill each other. But remember what you ...about self-control—when you

Have the guys put their letters in self-addressed envelopes that *you will mail* in six to eight weeks. (If you're the kind of person who often forgets to mail your mail, then put another leader in charge of this.) Tell the guys to seal the envelopes if they want to keep their letters private and to leave the envelopes unsealed if they would like you to read them before mailing.

## A Time for Peer Affirmation

The purpose of peer affirmation is to give teens an opportunity to practice the fine

**You'll need—**
• Paper
• Pens

art of uplifting and encouraging one another—as well as the fine art of receiving a compliment. Here are some guidelines to share with the guys—

> ➤ Sincerity, sincerity, sincerity
> ➤ Encouragement, encouragement, encouragement
> ➤ Consider pairing up with someone other than your best friend so you can strengthen another relationship. (If you choose the partners, keep this point in mind when making your selections.)

**quote**

"Initiation takes place over a period of years. It includes planned, institutional, accidental, incidental, and ritual rites of passage. A rite of passage is a part of initiation, not all of it, just as a bar mitzvah is only the beginning, not the whole, initiation of boys into manhood…Any educational structure that leads the boy through a social and personal journey of growth becomes an initiation experience."
—*Michael Gurian in* The Wonder of Boys
*(Tarcher/Putnam, 1996, page 151)*

However you handle peer affirmations, be *certain* you plan the details so everyone is included to the same degree. Being left out or underrepresented in this activity can have an adverse impact that is difficult to overcome. Leaders should be prepared with affirmations for each guy (that aren't being used during A Time For Leadership Affirmation) to use if necessary.

Happy are people of integrity, who follow the law of the Lord. Happy are those who obey his decrees and search for him with all their hearts. How can a young person stay pure? By obeying your word and following its rules.
—*from Psalm 119:1-2, 9, NLT*

Here are some ideas about how to handle peer affirmations—

**Affirmation chats**—*paired up, one-on-one, face-to-face communication*

Give the guys several minutes to affirm one another verbally with statements that begin with one or more of these phrases:

> ➤ You are… *(You're easy to get to know.)*
> ➤ You have… *(You have the ability to help everyone join in.)*
> ➤ I admire… *(I admire the way you seem comfortable in many different situations.)*
> ➤ I've noticed… *(I've noticed that you act friendly with all the guys, not just friends you usually hang with.)*

**Affirmation letters**—*paired off letter writing*

Have students spend some time writing a letter to a partner listing affirmations like those listed above. Give students an opportunity to read their letters when time is up or let them take the letters home to read later.

**Affirmation groups**—*multiple words of encouragement*

Divide students into groups of four or five. Instruct them to take just a few minutes to write down an affirmation for each guy in the group. When they're done, have the guys read their affirmations out loud to the group so everyone can be a part of the encouragement.

## A Time for Leader Affirmation

The purpose of leader affirmation is to demonstrate to each and every student that you notice him, you know him, you value him, and you're cheering for him.

**You'll need—**
• The determination to do this well
• Index cards (optional)
• Materials for affirmations, such as masculine-looking paper and envelopes (optional)

Here are some guidelines—

➤ Affirmations should be specific. No all-purpose, one-size-fits-all affirmations allowed. ("Your sense of humor helps me look at the bright side of hard situations," not, "You're such a great kid.")
➤ Affirmations should be accurate. (Research by calling a parent, relative, or friend if necessary.)
➤ Affirmations should be written down so the guys can keep them. (They'll read them many times!)

**◎ TIP**

**If your group is large, divide this responsibility among all the leaders, letting each one be in charge of affirming the guys he knows best.**

Here are ideas about what to do—

## Toasting

Bring up the guys individually and toast them in front of everyone. Depending on the size of your group, toasts can be as short as two or three sentences or as long as two or three minutes (but about the same for everyone).

Toasts should be accurate, specific, and relevant to the previous sessions. You are affirming, not complimenting. In other words, "Scott, tonight I want to toast you because you're such a wonderful long-distance runner," is a loser. "Scott, I want to toast you because of the way you greet new people who come to youth group. Your easy-going manner really makes them feel welcome," is a winner.

Prepare beforehand. Do not make these toasts on the spur of the moment. Have each toast written on an index card that you give to the student when the toast is finished. This says to each teen, "You are so important to me that I thought about you this week and planned what I want to say to you."

## Notes

Write a personal note of affirmation to each of your students during the week. Seal each letter in an envelope. During the evening, distribute the letters to the guys personally.

If there's any possibility of visitors, have a few extra letters available. Since it may be nearly impossible to pull together a personal letter for visitors, see the sample below for appropriate general wording, but make every effort to personalize the letters for your guests.

> Dear Jason,
>
> We're glad you came tonight. For the past couple of weeks, we've been discussing our God-created identity, sexual integrity, friendships, and other issues that are part of daily life. The most important and exciting thing we've discussed is the fact that God is interested in every part of our lives and that he has a plan and purpose for each of us. We hope you had fun tonight, and we'd love to see you again next week.
>
> Warmly,
>
> Jay Dearborn
> Youth Director

## A Time for Blessing

### Words of blessing

**You'll need—**
- **Gifts, one for each guy (optional)**
- **Pastor or other adult (see directions for details, optional)**

Throughout the Old Testament, the idea of passing a blessing down from one generation to another was a common part of helping boys transition to manhood. In I Kings 2:2-4 King David passes on a blessing to his son Solomon. He shares his dreams and hopes for Solomon as well as some cautions and admonitions.

We can use this idea of giving a blessing to help solidify the transition from boyhood to manhood. One by one, bring your guys to the front and communicate God's love, protection, and purpose for your students' lives, and *your* hopes and dreams for them. (Keep it short so this doesn't sound like a lecture!)

If you're toasting your teens, this can follow immediately after their affirmations, perhaps in the form of a prayer. The blessings should also be personal and specific instead of general.

## Gifts

Gift-giving will help make this event feel like a celebration for your guys. Because every youth group is so different (ages, maturity, number of students, interests, finances, depth of relationships) below you'll find several categories of gift ideas to launch your thinking.

Like the old truism says, "It's the thought that counts." This means that whether you spend pennies or dollars, whether you go the practical or the silly route, whether you wrap with fancy paper or lunch sacks, for maximum impact you need to carefully consider your choice of gifts.

If you present individualized gifts, the gifts should compliment individual personalities and interests. If you give the same gift to everyone, choose a gift with broadly based appeal. If you hate shopping or you feel paralyzed by the thought of choosing appropriate gifts, enlist the help of other leaders, adults or parents. You may also want to ask the girls in your youth group (those who know the guys reasonably well) for their ideas.

*Gifts for Christian Living*
- *The Message* (you can write a personal note inside the cover)
- New Testament (ditto)
- Devotional for guys
- Christian CD
- Journal and pen

*Practical Gifts*
- Tools
- Water bottle
- Work gloves
- Key chain

*Just-for-Fun/Childhood Retro Gifts*
- Pez dispensers and refill candies
- Nerf toys
- Squirt guns
- Silly putty

*Gifts for Hobbies and Interests*
- Guitar picks
- Trading cards
- Sports equipment (surfing wax, goggles, golf balls)
- Juggling balls

*Gifts with Symbolic Meaning*
- Carabiner—a metal ring with a spring-hinge on one side, used for mountan climbing. A symbol of staying connected to Jesus.
- Three-fold rope—a rope of three strands twisted together to remind your guys of the importance of quality friendships. "A cord of three strands is not quickly broken. (Ephesians 4:12)
- Flashlight—the guys are called to be lights in the world.
- Crescent wrench—an adjustable wrench to signify our ever-changing lives in Jesus.

## Pastoral prayer

Invite your senior pastor—or another adult who has a relationship or a special connection with your group—to join you for this session. Ask him to pray a special prayer of dedication, commitment, and blessing upon the guys.

## Group prayer

Involve students in the prayer and blessing time. Let volunteers pray for the group as a whole, as they move toward adulthood, as they live out their faith in their daily lives, as they work on sexual integrity and so forth.

Whatever options and activities you choose for this session, let your ultimate goal be that your guys have fun as they take one more step toward adulthood, toward mature faith, and toward becoming a man of God.

# Breaking Down the Wall

Make a list of words that describe you today.

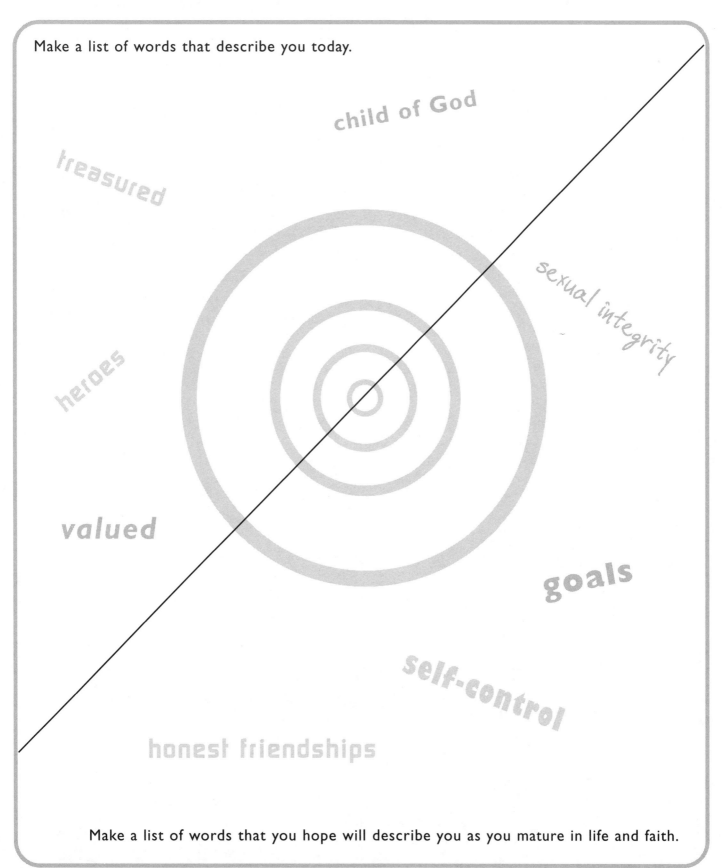

child of God

treasured

sexual integrity

heroes

valued

goals

self-control

honest friendships

Make a list of words that you hope will describe you as you mature in life and faith.

# Resources from Youth Specialties

## IDEAS LIBRARY
Ideas Library on CD-ROM 2.0
Administration, Publicity, & Fundraising
Camps, Retreats, Missions, & Service Ideas
Creative Meetings, Bible Lessons, & Worship Ideas
Crowd Breakers & Mixers
Discussion & Lesson Starters
Discussion & Lesson Starters 2
Drama, Skits, & Sketches
Drama, Skits, & Sketches 2
Drama, Skits, & Sketches 3
Games
Games 2
Games 3
Holiday Ideas
Special Events

## BIBLE CURRICULA
Creative Bible Lessons from the Old Testament
Creative Bible Lessons in 1 & 2 Corinthians
Creative Bible Lessons in Galatians and Philippians
Creative Bible Lessons in John
Creative Bible Lessons in Romans
Creative Bible Lessons on the Life of Christ
Creative Bible Lessons in Psalms
Downloading the Bible Kit
Wild Truth Bible Lessons
Wild Truth Bible Lessons 2
Wild Truth Bible Lessons—Pictures of God
Wild Truth Bible Lessons—Pictures of God 2

## TOPICAL CURRICULA
Creative Junior High Programs from A to Z, Vol. 1 (A-M)
Creative Junior High Programs from A to Z, Vol. 2 (N-Z)
Girls: 10 Gutsy, God-Centered Sessions on Issues
   That Matter to Girls
Guys: 10 Fearless, Faith-Focused Sessions on Issues
   That Matter to Guys
Good Sex
Live the Life! Student Evangelism Training Kit
The Next Level Youth Leader's Kit
Roaring Lambs
So What Am I Gonna Do with My Life?
Student Leadership Training Manual
Student Underground
Talking the Walk
What Would Jesus Do? Youth Leader's Kit
Wild Truth Bible Lessons
Wild Truth Bible Lessons 2
Wild Truth Bible Lessons—Pictures of God
Wild Truth Bible Lessons—Pictures of God 2

## DISCUSSION STARTERS
Discussion & Lesson Starters (Ideas Library)
Discussion & Lesson Starters 2 (Ideas Library)
EdgeTV
Every Picture Tells a Story
Get 'Em Talking
Keep 'Em Talking!
High School TalkSheets—Updated!
More High School TalkSheets—Updated!
High School TalkSheets from Psalms and Proverbs—Updated!
Junior High-Middle School TalkSheets—Updated!
More Junior High-Middle School TalkSheets—Updated!
Junior High-Middle School TalkSheets from Psalms
   and Proverbs—Updated!
Real Kids: Short Cuts
Real Kids: The Real Deal—on Friendship, Loneliness,
   Racism, & Suicide
Real Kids: The Real Deal—on Sexual Choices,
   Family Matters, & Loss
Real Kids: The Real Deal—on Stressing Out,
   Addictive Behavior, Great Comebacks, & Violence

Real Kids: Word on the Street
Small Group Qs
Have You Ever...?
Unfinished Sentences
What If...?
Would You Rather...?

## DRAMA RESOURCES
Drama, Skits, & Sketches (Ideas Library)
Drama, Skits, & Sketches 2 (Ideas Library)
Drama, Skits, & Sketches 3 (Ideas Library)
Dramatic Pauses
Spontaneous Melodramas
Spontaneous Melodramas 2
Super Sketches for Youth Ministry

## GAME RESOURCES
Games (Ideas Library)
Games 2 (Ideas Library)
Games 3 (Ideas Library)
Junior High Game Nights
More Junior High Game Nights
Play It!
Screen Play CD-ROM

## ADDITIONAL PROGRAMMING RESOURCES
*(also see Discussion Starters)*
Camps, Retreats, Missions, & Service Ideas
   (Ideas Library)
Creative Meetings, Bible Lessons, & Worship Ideas
   (Ideas Library)
Crowd Breakers & Mixers (Ideas Library)
Everyday Object Lessons
Great Fundraising Ideas for Youth Groups
More Great Fundraising Ideas for Youth Groups
Great Retreats for Youth Groups
Great Talk Outlines for Youth Ministry
Holiday Ideas (Ideas Library)
Incredible Questionnaires for Youth Ministry
Kickstarters
Memory Makers
Special Events (Ideas Library)
Videos That Teach
Videos That Teach 2
Worship Services for Youth Groups

## QUICK QUESTION BOOKS
Have You Ever...?
Unfinished Sentences
What If...?
Would You Rather...?

## VIDEOS & VIDEO CURRICULA
Dynamic Communicators Workshop
EdgeTV
Live the Life! Student Evangelism Training Kit
Make 'Em Laugh!
Purpose-Driven™ Youth Ministry Training Kit
Real Kids: Short Cuts
Real Kids: The Real Deal—on Friendship, Loneliness,
   Racism, & Suicide
Real Kids: The Real Deal—on Sexual Choices,
   Family Matters, & Loss
Real Kids: The Real Deal—on Stressing Out,
   Addictive Behavior, Great Comebacks, & Violence
Real Kids: Word on the Street
Student Underground
Understanding Your Teenager Video Curriculum
Youth Ministry Outside the Lines

## CLIP ART
Youth Group Activities (print)
Clip Art Library Version 2.0 (CD-ROM)

## ESPECIALLY FOR JUNIOR HIGH
Creative Junior High Programs from A to Z, Vol. 1 (A-M)
Creative Junior High Programs from A to Z, Vol. 2 (N-Z)
Junior High Game Nights
More Junior High Game Nights
Junior High-Middle School TalkSheets—Updated!
More Junior High-Middle School TalkSheets—Updated!
Junior High-Middle School TalkSheets from Psalms
   and Proverbs—Updated!
Wild Truth Journal for Junior Highers
Wild Truth Bible Lessons
Wild Truth Bible Lessons 2
Wild Truth Journal—Pictures of God
Wild Truth Bible Lessons—Pictures of God
Wild Truth Bible Lessons—Pictures of God 2

## STUDENT RESOURCES
Downloading the Bible: A Rough Guide to the
   New Testament
Downloading the Bible: A Rough Guide to the
   Old Testament
Grow for It! Journal through the Scriptures
So What Am I Gonna Do with My Life?
Spiritual Challenge Journal: The Next Level
Teen Devotional Bible
What (Almost) Nobody Will Tell You about Sex
What Would Jesus Do? Spiritual Challenge Journal

## DIGITAL RESOURCES
Clip Art Library Version 2.0 (CD-ROM)
Great Talk Outlines for Youth Ministry
Hot Illustrations CD-ROM
Ideas Library on CD-ROM 2.0
Screen Play
Youth Ministry Management Tools

## PROFESSIONAL RESOURCES
Administration, Publicity, & Fundraising (Ideas Library)
Dynamic Communicators Workshop
Great Talk Outlines for Youth Ministry
Help! I'm a Junior High Youth Worker!
Help! I'm a Small-Group Leader!
Help! I'm a Sunday School Teacher!
Help! I'm an Urban Youth Worker!
Help! I'm a Volunteer Youth Worker!
Hot Illustrations for Youth Talks
More Hot Illustrations for Youth Talks
Still More Hot Illustrations for Youth Talks
Hot Illustrations for Youth Talks 4
How to Expand Your Youth Ministry
How to Speak to Youth...and Keep Them Awake at
   the Same Time
Junior High Ministry (Updated & Expanded)
Make 'Em Laugh!
The Ministry of Nurture
Postmodern Youth Ministry
Purpose-Driven™ Youth Ministry
Purpose-Driven™ Youth Ministry Training Kit
So That's Why I Keep Doing This!
Teaching the Bible Creatively
A Youth Ministry Crash Course
Youth Ministry Management Tools
The Youth Worker's Handbook to Family Ministry

## ACADEMIC RESOURCES
Four Views of Youth Ministry & the Church
Starting Right
Youth Ministry That Transforms